# COOL JOBS

REY RABHAN

# MUSIC BUSINESS!

# COOL
# JOBS
## IN THE
BY JEFFREY RABHAN
# MUSIC
# BUSINESS!

inTune PARTNERS

Distributed by Hal Leonard Corporation

Published in 2013 by In Tune Partners
582 North Broadway
White Plains , NY 10603

Distributed by Hal Leonard Corporation
7777 West Bluemound Road
Milwaukee, WI 53213

Front cover photos (people clockwise from top left): courtesy of New York University; iStockphoto/thinkstock; Stockbyte.thinkstock; Creatas/thinkstock; iStockphoto/think-stock; Creatas/thinkstock; Emile Menasché; Ron Chapple Studios/thinkstock; Brand X Pictures/thinkstock; Brand X Pictures/thinkstock; (background image): iStockphoto/thinkstock. Back cover photo: Jacob Blumberg. Every reasonable effort has been made to contact copyright holders and secure permissions. Omissions can be remedied in future editions.

Printed in the United States of America

Editorial Director: Emile Menasché
Book Design: Jackie Jordan

Library of Congress Cataloging-in-Publication Data is available  upon request.

ISBN: 978-1-4584-2096-1

musicalive.com

*To Sadye, Dash and Tallulah—the "coolest job" of all.*

# CONTENTS

# ACKNOWLEDGMENTS

This book could not have been written without the help of many people. I'd like to thank my assistants and researchers Ben Norris and Russell Wagoner, my guru and editorial guide Emile Menasché, book designer Jackie Jordan, proofreader Rachel Borok, and give a special nod to everyone who interviewed for the book: They're all busy professionals, yet they took the time to share their own valuable experiences in the business, enriching the text, and, most important, offering the kind of insight that will be valuable to anyone trying to succeed in the music industry.

I owe my favorite jobs in the music business to Bob Guccione, Jr., Andrew Leary, Jeff Kwatinetz, and Clive Davis.

I'd also like to thank Swizz Beatz, Kevin Liles, Ryan Leslie, Steve Stoute, and Benny Blanco for being most gracious with their time in developing the next generation of music industry leaders.

Finally a word of special thanks goes to Michelle Branch, Kelly Rowland, Clive Davis, Jermaine Dupri, Nikki Mirasola, Walter and Barbara Rabhan, Jules Coleman, and the staff and faculty of the Clive Davis Institute of Recorded Music at New York University's Tisch School of the Arts.

## FOREWORD

# A WORD FROM JERMAINE DUPRI

**W**hen I first entered the music business a while back, it was a different world. When I formed So So Def Recordings, before Kriss Kross went multi-platinum and before I signed Bow Wow, the challenges facing an up-and-comer were very different from those you face on the scene today. But the main principle behind success in this music business—one constantly shaken by change—has remained consistently true: to succeed in the music industry, you need to *really know* the music industry.

You need to know, as I've learned through years of experience, how much work goes into making a record or charting a single. I've written and produced for folks like Usher and

Mariah Carey, and I've built many of my So So Def artists from scratch. I've been a winner at the GRAMMY Awards, the *Billboard* Awards, the BET awards, and the ASCAP awards. I can tell you this from experience: The hours are long and the work is tough, but each project starts the same. You need to know the world you're bringing your music into. You need to know your industry.

This book is monumentally important, because it helps you do just that. Right here in your hands, you have insider knowledge from people at the top of this business. This is unlike any other guide to the industry. It is practical, honest, and detailed to the point of providing you with your very next step as a student. You will walk away from this book with an understanding of the different occupations available in this business, which gives you a chance to find a fit for your unique talents.

Jeff Rabhan knows this industry inside and out. He is perfectly positioned to write a book to help you do the same, having managed artists through some of this business' most drastic shifts in technology and politics. He thinks two steps ahead of current trends and navigates artists' careers for long-term relevance.

As chair of New York University's Clive Davis Institute of Recorded Music, Jeff has mastered the challenge of teaching something that can't be trapped in the classroom. The music business is a living, breathing, feeling entity. To fully educate about this industry, you need to live in its ups and downs. Jeff has done just that. He is an active artist manager whose clients have garnered more than a dozen Grammy Awards. He brought every second of that experience and every ounce of his passion for teaching into the creation of this book.

This isn't a textbook meant to sit on your bookshelf. It's a roadmap that can guide you through your professional life in the music business. Now more than ever, we need forward-looking, big picture thinkers to shape the future of this industry. With new technology emerging every day, and new skills needed alongside it, now is your time to excel in the business of live and recorded music. Step one is always the same: know your industry. It starts right here.

Jermaine Dupri
*September 2012*
*Atlanta, Georgia*

## INTRODUCTION

# WELCOME TO THE BIZ

**W**hen I first began working in the music business, there were no books like this one. There were very few contemporary music programs at colleges and universities, and there were no roadmaps to help budding stars of the industry learn about the industry itself. In short, if you were lucky enough to get an entry-level job in the music business, you were going in only with the knowledge you possessed from your music collection and the hope that some executive would take you under their wing and teach you the ways of the world so as to avoid making horrible career mistakes. Your degree in most cases was not helpful, and there was little you could do to prepare for a career in the industry. It is my hope that this book changes much of that for you.

Many of you have an interest in this business but don't know where to begin. A number of you know what you want but have no idea how to prepare for it. This book will solve both of those issues by explaining how various sectors of the business operate so that you may best determine where your skills are suited. You may confirm that your desire to work at a record company in marketing is a great fit for you or conclude that you really would love to work in artist relations for a guitar company. The jumping off point is discovery!

You can use this book in two distinctly different ways: First, it can be used as an overview of the music industry that provides the knowledge you must have if you are interested in taking the next step towards a career in the business. Secondly, the book can help you plan a course of action; it will help you identify your interests, decide what to study in college (and which classes to take), pair you with potential careers, and help you determine what your personal strengths truly are.

This is not a general book written by an outsider. I have drawn upon my 20 years of experience in the music industry, as well as that of the many successful executives, artists, and veterans interviewed for this book in most sectors of the industry. You will get firsthand information from many of the people who are responsible for the artists you love, the songs you hear on the radio, and those who have shaped the modern music business from the stage to the classroom.

Turn the page and begin to explore what a job in the most exciting business in the world may look like for you.

# THE HISTORY OF THE MUSIC BUSINESS

**M**usic is without question one of the most exciting and powerful industries in the world. It's a multibillion-dollar business and the biggest names are recognized across the globe. Because of its adaptability to emerging forms of technology, the music industry has changed rapidly in its short history: In less than 70 years, it has gone from the sale of sheet music to digital song files! In that time the world has witnessed songs, musicians and performers never to be forgotten.

In many ways, the fundamental principle of the business of music has never changed; writing a great song and getting people to hear it has remained constant throughout music history. But everything else surrounding that core element has evolved with time, cultural change, technological advancements and shifts in public perception. There was a time when you couldn't see Elvis' hips on national TV without public outcry—less than 40 years later, you can see Lady Gaga in a meat dress on the MTV Video Music Awards.

## The Big Picture

While people have been making music for hundreds of years, the music business that we now know has existed for a relatively short time. Elements of the business have remained constant throughout—such as compelling people to listen to a certain artist and distributing music so that people can access it. In the very early stages of technology, the industry was based around singles; in other words, people bought one song at a time. Now, in the digital age, music has again become a business based largely around singles.

People get into this business because they love music—I think that's the one thing everyone in this industry has in common. But loving music is not enough. You should have an overall view of how the business works, what everyone else does, and how all of the pieces work together. To be successful, you need to understand the subtleties of all of the various positions within the industry. To avoid going into your future profession blindly, it is important to recognize your strengths and weaknesses, and use this knowledge to interpret how your personality may affect your career choice. Someone shouldn't become a doctor merely because they are interested in anatomy, right? Well, you shouldn't join the music business just because you're interested in music—there are many more things to consider first.

In the past, many of us inside the business learned about the industry and the various jobs within it in a hit-or-miss fashion, making plenty of mistakes along the way. But times have changed. Technology has allowed for more—and a more diverse range—of music business opportunities.

Let's take the last 70 years: Music has gone from the door-to-door selling of sheet music to jukeboxes, to singles and full-length albums on vinyl, to cassettes, to CDs, to down-loadable digital music. That's a lot of change for any industry in a short period of time. While emerging digital media may change the physicality of music, the principles behind its creation remain the same.

## THE EARLY STARS

Dating back to the great classical composers hundreds of years ago, and earlier still, music has always been (and remains) central to culture. Opera singers filled packed concert halls, the Prima Donnas of their day paving the way for today's Madonnas. These were the first live performing stars of the business. And although a lot of you might see classical music as boring, there were plenty of composers that were immersed in scandals because their music was considered too radical. In some cases, this music even had the ability to cause riots similar to how a hardcore or punk show might today. In a famous example from 1913, Igor Stravinsky's *The Rite of Spring* shocked and outraged a Parisian audience, causing fights and unrest in the concert hall. It doesn't matter if the audience is wearing tuxedos or studded leather jackets; music will always have the ability to evoke intense emotional responses from almost anyone at any time.

## FILM AND RADIO

The music business changed radically in the first half of the 20th century. From the days of DJs picking songs on payola (getting paid to play songs on the radio) to huge national conglomerates with stations in every big city, radio became (and remains) a crucial way that people discover music. Despite competition from other mediums—from digital radio to internet streaming sites—terrestrial radio remains central. In many ways, radio democratized music, allowing people from remote regions to access songs they would otherwise never have heard. When people couldn't afford to travel to a concert hall to see their favorite artist perform, they were able to sit around the radio and tune into the concert from their living room. Radio proved a critical step in bringing music to the people.

Emerging film technology created new opportunities for musicians and composers. With the advent of sound in film, composers could now create and sell their work for soundtracks, TV themes and more. Around this time, musical instruments went from a small-scale, handmade business to being manufactured on an industrial scale, putting instruments into far more people's hands.

# An Industry Is Born

Prior to the 1950s, the music business was based around sheet music and jukeboxes. In the '50s, the artists were often just vehicles for songs and publishers: The writers were really the drivers of the business. In many cases, it was the song itself selling, not a certain artist's version of that song.

## THE MOTOWN MODEL

Into the 1950s, the business experienced the rise of the record company—businesses that existed to produce and sell recordings. This meant a number of things. The record companies allowed for the creation of multiple departments that had not existed before: artist development, imaging, marketing, and others.

When Berry Gordy, Jr. founded Motown Records in 1960—best known for an artist roster that included Stevie Wonder, The Supremes, Smokey Robinson and many more—he created an incredibly successful model that would influence record company practices for decades to come.

The success of Motown brought to focus standard record company departments like radio promotion, artist development and publicity. It also set today's standards for the foundation of traditional distribution between labels, manufacturers and retail outlets. Along with these changes, strict controls were exercised over all aspects of a final product. The Motown model was seminal because the label did so much more than merely sell records: It became active in the creative process.

Finding talent and teaching artists the skills they needed was of paramount importance. Motown taught its artists how to perform, how to walk, how to talk—in essence everything required to shine in and out of the spotlight. In doing this, the Motown model created a sound, feel and personality not only for the artist but for the label itself.

## THE ARTISTS STEP FORWARD

The 1960s were powerful and interesting years for labels and publishers. The people who owned the recordings and copyrights to music began to profit heavily, and out of the sheet music world came songs that would live and breathe as recorded music. The result of this industry takeoff was the rise of the artist.

Understanding the public's affinity for celebrity musicians, labels helped spawn hugely successful careers of bands and singer/songwriters like Stevie Wonder, the Beatles and Bob Dylan. They were no longer just puppets for the labels or vehicles for the songs. They developed their own style, their own sound, their own songs and their own relationships with a fan base.

With the rise of the artist came a growing touring business. Headline artists started to become attractions who could play full-length concerts on their own—as opposed to the variety show performances of the 1950s, in which a number of bands would play a very limited amount of music each. If you want a better understanding of variety shows, check out The Wonders in the film *That Thing You Do!* (1996). A whole new set of jobs grew up around them: road managers, stage crew, promoters, sound engineers, people selling merchandise, making posters, and more.

The United States witnessed the first British Invasion, which showed that the music business was not provincial, but was instead a worldwide international force. As the '60s drew to a close, musicians had become images of and symbols for society. Artists had taken on a whole new cultural significance.

## MANAGERS AND STUDIOS

With the rising power of talent, artist representation became far more critical; one can look toward the importance of Brian Epstein with the Beatles and David Geffen—an agent turned manager—with Crosby, Stills and Nash. In the late '60s and early '70s, managers and artists had a more powerful role in the business as their presence in the marketplace overshadowed that of the record companies' own.

Along with other factors, managers forced record companies to create better business and financial arrangements, better deals, and better participation on behalf of their clients—changes which became industry standards that still exist today. This moment brought forward the reality of conflicting interests in the industry: There were different opinions (and sometimes disputes) over finances, creative vision, artistic direction and other matters.

In the '60s, recording studios became more important than ever before. As artists and their managers started to look for new sounds, they sought out talented record producers and recording engineers. Equipment manufacturers started to experiment with electronics to create new sounds, which in turn inspired new songs. That collaboration between equipment-makers and artists is even stronger today.

## THE TECHNOLOGICAL REVOLUTION

The 1980s were marked by a major technological shift that would again change the music business: the advent of the compact disc (CD). The CD injected tens of billions of dollars into the industry in a matter of years. People went out and purchased new music *in addition* to re-purchasing music that they had already owned on vinyl. This set off an explosion. The influx of cash caused record companies, staff and A&R departments to balloon in size, and the business increasingly became an international enterprise.

By the 1980s, music was arguably the most powerful medium in entertainment. International and cosmopolitan superstars began appearing in all forms of media, making them more exposed than the artists of earlier generations. With the advent of '80s media—such as MTV and the use of popular music in television commercials and advertisements—these huge artists became ubiquitous in our culture. There was no longer only the Beatles; there was Michael Jackson, Madonna, Whitney Houston, Bon Jovi and more.

During this time, the record companies experienced a resurgence of power. While artists were experiencing success previously unseen on such a wide level, record companies and radio stations controlled the business through a combination of cash and power, which fostered the advent of the celebrity record executive. A few label heads were as well known as the artists themselves—consider famous music moguls such as Clive Davis, Tommy Mottola and Quincy Jones.

**THE TIMES THEY WERE A-CHANGIN'**

The early 90s was a great time for music—managers, labels and artists alike were happy with their success. There seemed to be room for everyone in the industry: Hip-hop was taking off, stadium rock was huge and the independent music scene was burgeoning. Money and success were flowing widely. Then came the disruptive technology of the digital revolution. Nobody knew what the technology could bring, and the entire industry was unprepared for what these shifts would mean for the music business.

# It's a Whole New Biz

So where are we now? More than ever before, it is important that the industry finds and develops the next generation of executives and creative people. The demand for music is still incredibly strong: Great songs are as important in people's lives today as they ever have been. 150 years ago, the only way to listen to your favorite music was to hear it performed live or to perform it yourself—now you can hold a music library on a mobile phone or MP3 player and listen to songs virtually anywhere.

As it has been for decades, music is an essential part of radio and TV shows, movies, stage shows, advertisements and more. There are tons of ways to buy and listen to music; the soundtrack to your life now fits into your pocket. You can't walk into a supermarket without hearing music piping through the store's speakers. Go to a sporting event, and there's music for every occasion blaring through the sound system. Video games use music too. Some even let you be part of the rock band.

Music is part of our technologically-driven world in ways you may not think about. From phone ringtones to the start-up sounds your computer makes, music is always expanding into new markets and uncharted territories.

## THE PEOPLE BEHIND THE PRODUCT

When you see a great artist on TV, buy a song from iTunes or go to a great concert, you may not know that there are hundreds of people who make the final product possible. Throughout this book, we will examine a variety of roles within the music industry—some you may have heard of, some you probably haven't—and we'll hear from people at the top of their fields.

This is where you come in. Many of you readers are the industry's experts in the making, marketing, selling and performing of music. Whether using it as a guide or a reference, this book should help you form a clearer idea of the vast world of the music business, and where you might fit in.

# Music Education

Once there was one option for music education: conservatories. Today, there are music business programs, songwriting programs and technology programs, as well as traditional performance training. As college programs become more specialized, they require young students to have a good idea of their interests at a young age. The concept that artists, DJs, producers and engineers can go to a college program for training is extremely new. This book will help specify your interests within the music business so you can select the future training most beneficial to your success.

# Music Business Timeline

- **1870s:** Sheet music is the predominant form of musical reproduction, so much so that music publishers are not worried upon hearing about Thomas Edison's cylinder phonograph, invented in 1877. Rather than looking forward and investing an interest in the potential of a huge change, most sheet music publishers believe their business will remain dominant.

- **1889:** Louis Glass invents the "nickel-in-the-slot" machines, the 19th century equivalent to jukeboxes. Despite the technological advances in prerecorded cylinders, however, sheet music continues to dominate the market.

- **1890s:** methods of reproduction that depended on etched plates are replaced by recording into a phonograph onto a thick wax blank. Dynamics are difficult to capture in these recordings, and they require all instruments to be recorded simultaneously. When a musician plays very loudly, he/she throws off the dynamics of the song: There's a classic anecdote about Louis Armstrong having to stand way behind the rest of his band when recording because he was such a loud player!

■ **1890s:** Emile Berliner creates a system by which prerecorded cylinders can be reproduced on a large scale, making him the first person to envision the scope that the modern music business would have. In the late 1890s, the market for the Berliner discs becomes international.

■ **1901:** Berliner and Eldridge R. Johnson start the Victor Talking Machine Company. This leads major recording companies to make higher quality records.

■ **1920s:** As radio develops, it becomes extremely popular, causing the record industry to take a hit in sales and popularity.

■ **1925:** The first electrical recordings are issued by Victor and Columbia in the U.S.

■ **1936:** The first magnetic tape recording of a full symphony orchestra is produced. The industry soon follows suit and begins innovating with electrical means of audio reproduction.

■ **1956:** Stereo LPs become available in what proves a monumental breakthrough that changes sound recording. From the 1960s on, stereo virtually replaces mono.

■ **1960s-70s:** Following the LP, the cassette becomes the predominant form of recording and distribution. With time, LP sales decrease dramatically as cassette sales skyrocket.

■ **1964:** On February 7 the Beatles land at JFK Airport to 3,000 screaming fans, marking the beginning of the British Invasion.

■ **1977:** Fleetwood Mac releases their album *Rumors,* which sold 19 million copies in the United States alone. Songs like "Go Your Own Way" remain iconic today.

■ **1980s:** Compact Disc hardware and software launch in Japan in October 1982 and in England in March of 1983.

■ **1988:** Marks the first year in which CD sales outnumber vinyl sales. In addition, Michael Jackson, the self-proclaimed king of pop, is inducted into the Guinness Book of World Records for the most successful concert series of all time, the Bad World Tour. He is later recognized by Guinness as the most successful entertainer of all time.

■ **1996:** Record labels begin to produce "enhanced CDs," which have multimedia files added to new releases.

■ **1998:** MP3 players appear for downloaded audio.

■ **2001:** The first Apple iPod line is released on November 19, 2001, making digital music more portable than ever.

■ **2004:** Usher's album *Confessions* sets the record for most sales in the first week at 1.1 million copies. The album still holds as the best selling album of the 2000s. One popular journalist dubbed 2004 the "year of Usher."

■ **2005:** Pandora launches, using research from the Music Genome Project, which organizes songs in complex ways based on shared attributes. This is one of the earliest examples of the future prominence of streamed music.

■ **2006:** Spotify launches, creating a new business model for listening to music. Rather than having its users purchase songs, Spotify allows them to stream music.

■ **2011:** Adele's album *21* takes the world by storm, certified platinum 16 times in the UK. Her song "Rolling In The Deep" is the best selling digital song ever by a female artist.

■ **2012:** Katy Perry's album *Teenage Dream* surpasses Michael Jackson's *Thriller* for most number one hits on a single album.

## Looking Ahead

Now that you know some history, it's time to look at the music business as it is now and figure out where you might fit in. The questions in Chapter 2 are designed to help you find positions that might be suited to you, and the overview in Chapter 3 will give you a look at how various parts of the industry relate to one another. From there, you can explore each area of the music business in Chapters 4-14. Enjoy the journey!

# WHAT SHOULD YOU DO?

efore you begin exploring the various paths within the music industry, it's helpful to take a step back and assess your strengths and weaknesses. Doing so will allow you to get an idea of the areas in which you are most able to excel. This isn't to say that you can't try out different job specializations in order to discover what you do and don't like. The process of trial and error can often be a great learning experience. But going into the business with a strong understanding of your own assets will help you get on the right path quickly. In a world in which success can be achieved faster than ever, it always helps to be a step ahead. You should use this chapter as a guide; no one can decide the future of your career for you. The key is to get a general idea of places within the industry suited to your future success.

# Getting to Know You

The following questions will help you reflect on who you are and what you might like to do.

These questions are meant to get you thinking about how you can turn your interests into career opportunities; likewise, they should help you avoid turning your weaknesses into dead ends.

### GENERAL QUESTIONS

- Do you like working behind the scenes, or do you like being on the stage?
- Are you good with people?
- Are you very organized?
- Do you have a strong sense of business?
- Do you pay careful attention to detail?
- Are you more outgoing or more reserved?

**You may be more suited for a creative position if...**

- You are confident.
- You are independent.
- You are a risk taker.
- You think outside the box.
- You are passionate.
- You are curious.
- You are intuitive.
- You like to be challenged.

■ You are imaginative.

■ You are optimistic.

■ You are motivated by a task, not the reward.

■ You are expressive.

**You may be more suited for a business-oriented position if...**

■ You prefer structure.

■ You are organized.

■ You are focused.

■ You are goal-oriented.

■ You are responsible and reliable.

■ You are detail-oriented.

■ You are good at networking and building relationships.

■ You are disciplined.

■ You are adept at assessing risks.

■ You are comfortable with decision-making.

If you're a mix of these traits—as many people are—there are plenty of positions requiring diverse or unconventional skill sets, too!

# Finding Your Field

You can also use this question and answer survey to narrow down your choices. Here, we've broken possible jobs down into three categories: creative, business and both.

### CREATIVE CAREERS

■ Do you like spreading the word about music, products and people you enjoy?

■ Do you have a large network of friends and colleagues? Would you be good at building one?

■ Do you have a good ear for hearing the minor details of songs?

■ Are you knowledgeable about different types of instruments?

■ Are you a gifted singer, instrumentalist or musician?

■ Are you a tastemaker?

■ Do you stay up to date on all new digital platforms, software, etc.?

■ Do you enjoy writing? Are you a good writer?

## BUSINESS CAREERS

■ Do you like traveling?

■ Are you good at planning itineraries for trips?

■ Do you enjoy listening to new music and checking out new artists?

■ Are you a logical thinker?

■ Are you interested in the law?

■ Do you enjoy taking leadership roles in projects?

■ Are you good at balancing multiple projects?

■ Are you good at planning for the future?

■ Are you eager to become well-versed in all aspects of the music industry?

## HYBRID CAREERS

■ Do you hope to own your own business one day?

■ Are you good at developing creative but realistic ideas?

■ Do you have a wide knowledge of music that covers

different genres and time periods?

- Are you good at networking and building meaningful relationships?
- Do you have relationships with people on either extreme (creative and business) to assure you that your business is both grounded and exciting?

## What Your Survey Answers Tell You

How do these qualities fit within the industry? Below are some examples of how you can connect your talents and interests with specific types of jobs. Remember—these are just a few options! The music industry has plenty of jobs for people from all backgrounds and with different skill sets and interests.

**Are you good at identifying talent? Do you like finding new bands before they've become popular?**

A&R (Artist and Repertoire: talent scouting and development), independent record label owner

**Do you go to a lot of concerts?**

A&R, tour manager, sound engineer, show designer

**Are you active on social media? Do a lot of people like following your tweets and Facebook updates?**

Marketing, publicity, blogger

**Do you like working with computers and technology?**

Producer, mixer, mastering engineer, software developer, app developer

**Do you like writing?**

Journalist, blogger, educator, publicist, copywriter

**Are you interested in accounting or legal issues?**

Attorney, accountant, business manager

**Are you good at convincing others of your ideas?**

Marketer, publicist, senior level executive

**Do you find yourself explaining the technical aspect of music to your friends?**

Teacher, arts administrator, demonstrations, instrument lessons and clinics, producer, engineer

**Do you have a wide knowledge of music that spans different genres and time periods?**

Professor, blogger, journalist, DJ

**Do you enjoy taking leadership roles in volunteer projects?**

Philanthropist, music charity, business manager or any leadership/executive role

**Do you like being on the road or planning travel?**

Tour manager, touring musician, booking agent, roadie, instrument technician

**Are you good at multi-tasking and communicating efficiently and effectively?**

Manager, agent, executive

**Do people look to you to introduce them to new music?**
DJ, blogger, A&R, music supervisor, critic

**Do you have a good ear for hearing the minute details of songs?**
Producer, engineer, mixer, mastering engineer, arranger

**Do you hope to own your own business one day? Are you good at developing creative but feasible ideas?**
Label owner, manager, studio owner

**Do you like spreading the word to your friends about upcoming concerts?**
Venue marketing, events promotion, publicity

## Looking Ahead

Remember, these questions aren't a test and they're not designed to lock you into any kind of job. But the more honest you are with yourself while answering, the better this exercise will help you choose what to study and where to look for your first job in the music business. We'll take a look at some options in the next chapter.

# THE MARKETPLACE

**T**he music industry is in many ways a synchronized dance. Though its numerous parts may at times seem unrelated, the various jobs within the industry interact to create a final product that (when executed correctly) appears seamless.

The process is very linear, in the sense that there are certain things that must happen in a specific order before other things can happen. Because of this linear project flow, people in different sectors often need to know how other areas work. It's not unusual for people to work in many different areas in music during their career. There are overlapping skill sets, and it's important to know how many different specializations operate.

People in music tend to be multi-facited generalists rather than specialists. Despite the casual feel of music in general, the old image of the music business as one big party is not really an accurate depiction of the way things work. There are benchmarks that must be met to set certain things in motion.

One fantastic truth in the music industry is that nearly every person in the business loves music—I don't know many other industries in which that holds true. Every person, regardless of his/her specialization in the industry, has a story about music and why they became involved in it.

This shared passion fosters a level of understanding and camaraderie amongst relative strangers that binds them in a fraternal way. There's shared curiosity about popular culture, trends, media, and a desire to tap into the emotional elements that music underscores in people's lives. There's a large number of business-minded people in the industry who are musicians themselves with various skill levels. This business is so vibrant because it is made up largely of expressive people.

The industry attracts creative people from all walks of life—be it fashion, design, photography or otherwise. It's a fertile ground for artistic people, filled with opportunities for those with creative visions. Though the music industry often appears to be casual and without formalities, competition is fierce. If you're looking to escape a corporate environment, this could be the job for you. Corporate mergers have eradicated some of the casual culture the industry has made famous. There's still more room for personal expression than in most other organizations though—substance over style is the ticket to fitting in. Rather than suits and ties, you can have tattoos, jeans, and earrings.

Working in the music industry is an exciting and exhilarating opportunity to be a part of something that extends worldwide. It affords you the opportunity to see the world, create a creative product that lasts forever and contribute to the growth of something that starts off local and becomes an international phenomenon. It's a business where anything is possible—the kid from a small town can end up managing the biggest pop act in the country, or even become the biggest pop act.

## Record Labels

Record labels sign, develop and market artists. They scout new talent, sign artists and bands to recording contracts, oversee the recording of the music, then release and market that music to the public. When you purchase a CD, you may not realize how many different people contributed to the final product. From the design of the album artwork to the process behind getting a song to play frequently on the radio, there was someone at the label responsible for every aspect of the final product that you experience. There are people that have to put the music into a sellable format (whether CD, digital file, or vinyl record), create the packaging, manufacture copies, distribute the music to stores and websites, market the release and more.

In Chapter 4, you will get a more detailed look at the world of record labels and an idea of what steps you can take toward getting a job at a label.

### RECORD LABEL JOBS

Below is a brief list of the various jobs and departments that exist within record labels.

- President / chief executive officer
- Senior level administration positions (GM, business affairs, accounting)
- A&R
- Marketing / branding
- Sales
- Radio promotion
- Publicity
- Art department
- New media
- Video
- Licensing
- International department
- Executive assistant
- IT (information technology)

# Music Publishing

Music publishing is the business of acquiring, licensing, administering, protecting and exploiting musical compositions through their copyrights. Publishers also collect royalties on behalf of the songwriter. With performance royalties, mechanical royalties and synchronization royalties, the business of music publishing assures that when a songwriter's composition is used somewhere, he/she is receiving payment for that use. Aside from financial concerns, however, music publishers are also responsible for bringing together a songwriter's composition with an artist that is suited to perform it. In other words, when you hear a major hit on the pop charts, it's likely that a music publisher arranged for that composition to be sung by that artist. Many artists do not write their own songs, so they seek out publishers in order to get hit material to record and perform.

## MUSIC PUBLISHING JOBS

To give you an idea of the different areas within music publishing, below is a brief list of the various jobs that exist in this field.

- Chief executive officer (CEO)/ Chief financial officer (CFO)
- Legal
- Senior level team (head of business affairs, head of creative, head of copyrights and administration, head of marketing)
- Creative
- Synchronization (pitches and licenses music for film and TV)
- Marketing
- A&R
- Administrators
- International department
- Public relations (PR)
- Executive publicist
- Copyright, administration, royalties, collections

- Staff writers
- Executive assistant
- IT (information technology)

# Music Distribution

Music distribution companies are responsible for shipping and getting physical and digital songs stocked and re-ordered at major retail outlets. When you enter a store that sells music, the merchandise that you see didn't just end up there—it went through a strategic process during which many people decided where the music should be sold, how many units would need to be distributed, and how the music should be presented at those stores.

## MUSIC DISTRIBUTION JOBS

Music distributors are responsible for predicting how many units will be sold in retail outlets—they don't want you to go to a store and find that the CD is sold out, but they also don't want to have boxes and boxes of untouched material sitting in a store's warehouse. So what types of jobs are available in distribution? See below.

- President
- Marketing
- Business and legal affairs
- Accounting and royalties
- Label partner and relations
- Acquisitions
- Manufacturing

# Music Production

Production entails everything related to the physical recording, engineering, mixing and mastering of the music. The people involved in the production of any given recording are responsible for what you actually hear when listening to a song or album. The bass in a hip-hop song, the twang in a country song, the background vocals in a pop song—these are all recorded, manipulated and perfected by those working in music production.

## MUSIC PRODUCTION JOBS

Within production, many jobs can be done either independently or as part of an organization. Below are some of the many jobs within this field.

- Producing
- Recording engineer
- Mixing engineer
- Mastering
- Post-production engineer
- Broadcasts
- Remixing engineer
- Gear technicians
- Production assistant
- Assistant engineer
- Software editor (ProTools/Logic)
- Studio manager / owner
- Acoustic consultant

# Industry Organizations

Ranging from performing rights societies to industry-sponsored organizations and charities, these are groups that work on behalf of artists, writers, performers and more. They provide employment opportunities and networking opportunities, as well as various kinds of professional support.

## PROMINENT MUSIC INDUSTRY ORGANIZATIONS

The list below provides some of the larger entities, but you should research any organizations that may be related to your area of interest.

- ASCAP (American Society of Composers, Authors, and Publishers)
- BMI (Broadcast Music, Inc.)
- SESAC (Society of European Stage Authors and Composers)
- NARAS (National Academy of Recording Arts and Sciences)
- MusicCares
- MEIEA (Music and Entertainment Industry Educator's Association)
- A2IM (American Association of Independent Music)
- RIAA (Recording Industry Association of America)
- AES (Audio Engineering Society)
- NAMM (National Association of Music Merchants)
- NAfME (The National Association for Music Education)

# Media

Media jobs in the music industry involve publicity for various aspects of the business. Whether through newspapers, magazines, television, radio or another form, those working in the media are responsible for disseminating information about artists, performers and a host of other people.

## MEDIA JOBS

The creative outlets for those working media jobs are extensive. And now, with so many blogs, websites, e-zines and social media networks, there is a greater ability than ever before to have a part in the expansive media industry.

- Journalist
- Editor
- Copy editor
- Layout / design
- Photographer
- Photo editor
- Creative director
- Style editor
- Illustrator
- Publisher
- Broadcaster (talk show)
- DJ
- Blogger
- Radio: events, sales, marketing, promotions, sponsorships, merchandise
- Social media marketing

- Fan clubs
- Video director
- Video producer
- Video commissioner

# Music Education

Whether teaching piano to students at a conservatory, teaching the history of Southeast Asian music at a university, or directing a high school marching band, educators have a wide range of expertise about music that they share with students in a meaningful way. The paths to a music education job vary. Some educators have a Ph.D. in music, some have extensive experience working in the music industry and others have a strong performance background without any formal college education.

## EDUCATION JOBS

There is a wide range of opportunities within the music education sector based on your interests and abilities, and it's a great way to introduce your passion and experience to others who are excited to learn about them.

- Professor—Conservatory/performance
- Professor—Technology / production
- Professor—Music business
- Professor—History and criticism
- Professor—Ethnomusicology
- Music teacher in elementary, middle and high school
- Freelance music teacher

- Arts administrator
- Grant writer
- Curator
- University events/concert series manager

# Events

Perhaps by now you're starting to realize that each time you attend a concert, many different elements went into its planning, preparation and execution. Positions in the events side of music vary widely, but they are all in some way responsible for bringing together a great live performance. When you see the stage lighting and props and you hear the quality of the sound, you should recognize that there was someone on the live events side of the business who put it together. There's someone to make sure the artist is in the right city on the right day, someone who decides which venues are right for which artists and even someone who makes sure the guitars are tuned correctly!

## EVENTS JOBS

The live music business has become more important than ever in recent years, providing opportunities on both the local level and on regional, national and international tours. Here are a few key jobs:

- Agent
- Promoter
- Booker
- Tour manager
- Sound engineer

- Instrument technician
- Touring musician
- Facilities manager
- Lighting technician
- Show designer
- Stage building and design
- Merchandise sales
- Artist assistant

# Owning Your Own Business

Small business owners and self-employed individuals make up a huge segment of the music industry. The potential for entrepreneurial jobs within the industry is greater than ever, and much of the innovation occurring in the music space is a result of these self-employed individuals. Working in this sector means that you're able to turn great ideas into great products; these individuals think of solutions where they see problems and are constantly creating smarter, more efficient ways of handling business.

### ENTREPRENEURIAL JOBS

Below is a brief list to give you an idea of some of the options that exist—there are plenty more entrepreneurial opportunities out there though, many of which you can carve out for yourself.

- Managers
- Independent label owners
- Specialty retail shop owners

- Studio owners
- Artist
- Music supervisor
- Startup / business owner
- Blogger
- Philanthropy
- Music instruction (teaching, vocal coaching, etc.)
- Jingle writer
- Composer

# Technology

This area is an exciting and constantly evolving segment of the industry that is redefining delivery systems and connections between fans and artists. Those working in technology startups often combine an entrepreneurial spirit with technological savvy in order to create a product that is new, exciting and hopefully game-changing. Programs that you use (like iTunes, Spotify, Pandora and PledgeMusic) have large teams of people working for them, ranging from those who think of new ideas and directions for the company, to those who keep the programs functioning and operating seamlessly.

## TECHNOLOGY JOBS

This field is growing rapidly and has endless potential for new, young talent. Here are just a few of the jobs that are popular now, but many of these positions didn't even exist a few years ago, and it's a good bet that new positions will emerge as people come up with new ways to create, perform and share music.

- App development
- Software engineer
- Web developer
- Graphic designer
- IT
- Coder
- Copywriter
- Database manager

# Musical Instrument Industry

Without talented manufacturers and marketers who distribute intelligently designed equipment, that guitar you play and that recording software you use would not be possible. Working in the musical instrument field (known in the industry as "MI") can entail responsibilities that range from the physical construction of handmade guitars, to the development of the latest ProTools upgrades. Also, when you see your favorite musicians using a specific brand in their performances and videos, chances are there was someone in this industry who helped create that brand partnership; it isn't by chance that certain superstars use certain brands.

## INSTRUMENT AND EQUIPMENT DEVELOPMENT JOBS

Like other areas of music technology, the field of instrument and equipment making can undergo change very quickly. But it also has a traditional side. In other words, some people still make instruments using materials and techniques that go back centuries, while other use the latest digital technology.

And sometimes, they both work for the same company! Here are a few currently popular instrument and equipment jobs.

- Branding and marketing
- Software designer
- Industry outreach
- Demonstrations
- Artist relations
- Instrument and equipment design and creation
- Gear and equipment rep.

## Looking Ahead

As you can see, there really are many different jobs within the music industry. And as you'll learn by exploring further, many of these positions are connected to one another. You may be a producer who also plays concerts, or a marketing person who has a knack for A&R, or a lead singer with a great head for managing you own (and other) careers. In the end, it's up to you to define your own career (that's true whether you're in the music business or any other field). There's no reason you can't use your talents in a range of different ways. Keep that in mind as you look through the rest of this book.

# RECORD LABELS

I t doesn't matter if you work at a major record company with thousands of employees worldwide or if you work at an independent label run out of a basement; working at a record label is all about finding, marketing and selling music. This is true whether you're working in jazz, classical, heavy metal, pop or any other genre. You may be a publicist at a hip-hop label, but your job is still similar to the publicist at a country label.

The skill sets necessary to be successful within a record label are not specific to any given musical genre or label size: Once you develop your professional skills, you'll be able to use them within any number of creative cultures. Although the people may differ from label to label, the tasks that they perform are often very similar. The core of the job revolves around selling new products to people—that will never change, regardless of the format in which the music is sold (MP3, CD, vinyl or whatever else may develop). The fundamentals will always remain the same. We don't know what tomorrow will bring, but we do know that when tomorrow comes, you're still going to need to market and sell artists.

## Major and Independent Labels

Record labels were once only big companies, but today there's room in the musical spectrum for all sizes and types—from multinational corporations to one-person bedroom operations.

The two overarching categories that are used to describe labels are "major" and "independent" (or "indie"). As the names imply, major labels are much bigger in size, both in the amount of people they staff, and in the amount of artists on their roster. Indie labels tend to have far fewer people working for them, and their artist rosters tend to be smaller. Though there are some exceptions, there is also a difference between the type of music generally found on major labels versus indie labels. When you think of radio hits and Top 40 songs, these artists are more often than not associated with major labels, whereas experimental, alternative and other non-pop forms of music are usually found on niche-oriented indie labels.

The culture of record labels may be casual, but the responsibilities are serious. It's a collaborative environment that requires cooperation between individuals and departments in order to bring any product to market. At major labels, there's more room for different personalities and backgrounds—it's a diverse group of people. At small labels, you'll find much more like-minded, genre-specific people that take a more unified approach to business. You'll find less bureaucracy and less formality at smaller labels. At a major label, you'll most likely work within a department that has a specific function, whereas at an independent label, you're more likely to be a jack-of-all-trades and help out in every area that you can.

Now is a volatile time for the industry, but volatility creates opportunity. With the disruptive technology of the internet, record labels have undergone a seismic shift. That isn't to say that there is no opportunity within record labels today or in the future; the function of certain jobs will just continue to change with advances in technology. The future of record labels will depend on people who are constantly searching for the next big idea—people who don't only try to navigate through current trends, but who predict and help shape them. Record labels have adapted to the shift from vinyl to tapes, tapes to CDs, and CDs to MP3s: It's going to be up to young innovators like you to decide what the next step is going to be and how the music industry is going to react to it. When file sharing began to take off, record labels were lost. They knew of no way to cope with illegal downloading. Since then, they have developed various strategies and new methods of attaining revenue, but it took the efforts of people who didn't simply lament the demise of the industry to rise above illigal downloading. It took innovative people willing to see the shift as a challenge to overcome—merely the result of an industry so closely connected with the ever-changing world of technology.

# Label Departments

Whether you're working for a big company or a small one, a record label has a number of different departments, each with a job to do. At big labels, each department can have many employees, from entry-level workers to executives. At smaller labels, one or two people may do multiple jobs and report directly to upper management. But either way, the work performed by each of the following departments must get done for a label to be successful.

## A&R

In an artist and repertoire career your primary concern is finding new talent, signing new talent, and providing or locating material and songs for existing talent. This includes organizing recording sessions, hiring producers, and ultimately being responsible for the final musical product.

**Are you ready to...**
- Spend long hours in the recording studio?
- Search for unknown artists and talent?
- Develop a network of songwriters, producers and publishers?
- See lots of live music?
- Make important creative decisions?

**It helps to have...**

- A seasoned ear and eye for talent.
- The ability to understand trends in public tastes.
- An eye for creative potential.
- An ability to match songwriters and producers with artists—the ability to make smart pairings.

**In high school you can...**

- Stay updated on new music trends, styles and genres.
- Familiarize yourself with the people who wrote, produced, mixed and mastered big records.
- Study all genres of music, not just your favorites.
- Listen to older records—as well as new ones—to get an understanding of the history of sound.

## MARKETING/BRANDING

Those who work in marketing and branding come up with innovative and commercially viable ways to present an artist to the public. Whether through imaging, social media, merchandise or other means, the marketing and branding team is responsible for making sure that word gets out to as many people as possible about an artist.

**Are you ready to...**

- Create awareness campaigns for unknown artists?
- Identify the target audience for an artist?
- Create the portal used to communicate to that audience?
- Contribute to the overall branding and awareness of the artist?

**You should...**

- ■ Understand consumer habits.
- ■ Be able to find innovative and creative ways of presenting a product or idea.
- ■ Be a strong problem solver.
- ■ Have strong research and critical thinking abilities.

**In high school you can...**

- ■ Pay attention to how bands and brands are advertised and how they interact.
- ■ Study how celebrities and artists present themselves in photographs and interviews.
- ■ Use social media (Twitter and Facebook) to see how bands attract followers.

## SALES

Responsible for soliciting and educating retail outlets about upcoming releases and ultimately helping to determine—with the buyers—how many units to place in the initial order (IO). Sales is responsible for analyzing and understanding all of the different factors and signals that may influence a unit's marketability and sales potential.

**Are you ready to...**

- ■ Spread excitement and potential success for upcoming releases?
- ■ Work closely with manufacturing plants as well as retail outlets?
- ■ Insure the flow of product?

**You should have...**

- The ability to gather and interpret qualitative and quantitative information.
- Strong forecasting instincts and confidence in those instincts.
- Strong cultural sensibilities and great understanding of the retail marketplace.

**In high school you can...**

- Take all of the business classes available.
- Spend as much time as possible in record stores to understand how albums are priced and positioned.
- Familiarize yourself with the Soundscan system, which is the official means of tracking music sales in the United States.

**INSIDE STORY**

**RICK SACKHEIM**
Executive VP
Island Def Jam

*"Times change, styles of music become in fashion and out of fashion, and an expert can move with the times and with the different changes that take place in music yearly or monthly. You have to be able to ride that wave and really understand the marketplace; you can't dictate to the market, but instead have to ride the market."*

## RADIO PROMOTION (NATIONAL AND LOCAL)

Radio promotion serves as a conduit between music companies and radio stations: for promotions, events, show sponsorships, concert presentations and more.

When you listen to the radio, the songs aren't haphazardly chosen; they're brought to you largely by the efforts of those in radio promotion, who help convince radio stations to play certain songs based on marketable stories about the artist or recording.

**Are you ready to...**
- Travel extensively around the country?
- Spend a lot of time promoting music to program directors and music directors at radio stations?
- Work in a high-pressure environment?
- Work closely with artist managers?

**It helps to...**
- Be a high-energy individual with an outgoing personality.
- Understand and interpret how the music charts work and how playlists are developed.
- Understand the complex political environment of how songs are added to and maintained on radio playlists.

**In high school you can...**
- Listen to all formats of radio (FM, Satellite, Internet).
- Attend station-sponsored events and concerts.
- Intern at a radio station.
- Become a high school representative for your favorite local station.

## PUBLICITY

A publicist helps create and present an artist's image and personality to the public via all forms of media and public appearances. They are responsible for creating all biographic materials and approving all images and statements for public consumption. When you see your favorite artist give a press release, chances are a publicist either wrote it or approved it.

**Are you ready to...**

- Constantly pitch your artists to editors, writers and TV show bookers?
- "Spin" all situations into positive press coverage?
- Craft long-term awareness campaigns?
- Hire photographers, videographers and social media experts to execute plans?

**You should be...**

- Even tempered and able to work with all types of personalities.
- Good at assessing the strengths and weaknesses of individuals.
- Able to handle crises.
- Able to present ideas and personalities in a creative and commercially appropriate way.
- A good writer.

**In high school you can...**

- Pay close attention to how artists are portrayed in the media.
- Get involved in promoting and publicizing school events (battle of the bands, talent shows, etc.).
- Try to get the local media to cover something that you're involved in.

## ART DEPARTMENT

Oversees and creates logos, packaging artwork and all materials related to commercially released products. This person works closely with artists to interpret their personal vision and complement their music in a visual way.

**Are you ready to...**

■ Visualize musical concepts and put them into a marketable form?

■ Design all promotional materials for an artist, including posters, flyers and much more?

■ Collaborate with artists on their artistic vision?

**You should have...**

■ Skills in photography, editing and graphic design.

■ A pictorial mind; the ability to translate musical concepts into artistic images.

**In high school you can...**

■ Take graphic design and art classes.

■ Design album artwork and flyers for your friends' bands.

■ Make posters for upcoming school events.

■ Get involved in the yearbook and other school publications.

## NEW MEDIA

New Media oversees and directs social media strategies for companies and artists alike. This department works closely with artists and management to reach the existing fan base and develop new fan bases in both online and offline communities.

**Are you ready to...**

- Develop relationships on a corporate level with a variety of companies, from social networking sites to major retail stores and everything inbetween?
- Envision how online platforms can be used to reach millions of fans on an international stage?
- Stay current with technological advances and use them in order to promote musical ideas and people?

**You need to...**

- Have a strong understanding of social media through your own personal use of the platforms.
- Have a command of all current media and have an eye for upcoming trends.
- Balance the creative and the technological and be equally comfortable talking to an artist as to a technology developer.

> ### INSIDE STORY
> **JEREMY WELT**
> **New Media Executive**
>
> *"If you're going to help direct artists' social media sites, the artists need to be able to tell that you understand their art. It doesn't matter how good your ideas are; you have to put your head in the mind of the artist. They're emotional beings, and they want to feel like you understand that crazy emotional feeling."*

- According to Jeremy Welt, formerly the Senior Vice President of New Media at Warner Brothers, "You need to be someone who spends a lot of time understanding, identifying and empathizing with consumer behavior. You also need to have a continuing commitment to hands-on experience, meaning that you can't be in a deal talking about the rate of YouTube plays unless you have a strong understanding of YouTube through your own personal use of the site."

**In high school you can...**

■ Follow the Twitter feeds of successful social media entrepreneurs.

■ Analyze the social media strategy of artists that you respect: See how they present themselves, how they interact with fans, and what their followers respond to most.

■ Run your high school's Facebook, Twitter or YouTube channel.

## VIDEO COMMISSIONER

The video commissioner recommends directors, then oversees the budget, production and editing of a music video, much like a movie producer oversees the filming of a movie. They are also responsible for servicing the video to different outlets—MTV, Fuse, VH1, etc.—and promoting these videos to get them played.

**Are you ready to...**

■ Work closely with production companies, directors and editors?

■ Spend long hours on filming sets, which includes traveling to various locations?

■ Sift through multiple video treatments to help determine what the best fit is for the artist, both in terms of idea and director?

**It helps to...**

■ Have production experience.

■ Understand line-item production budgets.

■ Have a good eye for visual detail.

■ Understand the particular attributes and styles that make an artist look favorable.

**In high school you can...**

■ Shoot your friends' music videos and help them with editing.

■ Watch music videos and analyze the different components that make them interesting.

■ Take television and post-production classes.

## LICENSING

Market and promote catalog (which is a collection of compositions/songs) to film, television, commercial and other licensing outlets, to negotiate fees for usages and to support the promotion and marketing of new artists via tie-ins and soundtrack opportunities.

**Are you ready to...**

■ Pitch your song catalog to networks, studios, music supervisors and corporations?

■ Look for unconventional opportunities for music placements?

■ Negotiate fees in a highly competitive environment?

**You should...**

■ Know your catalog extremely well to be able to find smart placement for material.

■ Be able to recognize good pairings for artists

and projects.

■ Realize which artists are willing to license their material and which ones aren't, then finding the right placement for them.

**In high school you can...**

■ Pay attention to the music that's played in your favorite TV shows, as well as the advertisements during those shows.

■ Pitch bands from your school to local businesses for TV/radio commercials.

■ Develop strong research skills.

## INTERNATIONAL DEPARTMENT

Most record labels sell music all over the world, and some have departments that specifically oversee this aspect of their business. They are responsible for coordinating the promotional and release schedules of artists in multiple territories outside of the United States, in addition to explaining the differences in approach to the marketing and sales of music in other countries to the artist and artist's team.

**Are you ready to...**

■ Travel extensively around the world?

■ Work off-hours due to time differences?

■ Serve as an ambassador for your company and your artists?

■ Organize promotional and release schedules concurrently in multiple territories?

**You should be...**

- Marketing-minded; able to find out different ways to market the same product differently within different countries.
- Culturally aware and receptive to an extensive range of cultures.
- Willing to learn how to do the same task many different ways.
- Knowledgeable of how the media functions in major territories around the world.

# Senior Level Positions

How do all these departments work together? That's the job of senior management—the people who run the company and make the decisions that affect the overall direction of the business. According to Angelica Cob-Baehler, Executive Vice President of Marketing at Epic Records, being in a senior-level role at a record company is like being the head coach of a sports team:

"I sit down with the team and help craft the plays, then help execute the plays. I try to stay out of minutiae. Every once in a while, if someone needs special help or attention, I'll jump in. But it's important to maintain a big picture view of what our goals are, while also being able to get in the trenches and get your hands dirty. The most interesting aspect of the job is getting to know an artist to the core and really assisting them and communicating to the world what their vision is."

Senior management jobs include the following:

## PRESIDENT / CEO

The president/CEO holds the top job at the company, overseeing all aspects of the record company. He/she is responsible for maintaining the corporate culture and developing a long-term vision.

**Are you ready to...**

- Be ultimately responsible for the success or failure of a major company?
- Oversee all aspects of the business?
- Maintain relationships with artists and artist representatives?
- Publicly represent the company?

**You should be...**

- Someone with an understanding of both creative and corporate cultures.
- A great communicator.
- Someone who can recognize executive talent in building the company's team.
- Someone who has no trouble making tough decisions.
- Experienced! This is not an entry-level job. You should be willing to work your way up.

**To prepare, you can...**

- Run your own business. Believe it or not, many of the industry's giants started by creating a small business in high school or college, where they learned the basic of budgets, marketing and sales.

■ Have extensive work experience in the music industry or a related field.

■ Serve as president for one of your school clubs.

■ Read books about great executives in the music industry. Some of the greatest examples include Clive Davis (Columbia, Arista, J Records), David Geffen (Asylum, Geffen, DGC), Ahmet Ertegun (Atlantic) and Berry Gordy (Motown).

## Looking Ahead

The record business will continue to change as technology alters the ways people buy and listen to music. But many of the roles mentioned above are important in other areas of the music business. In fact, as you read on, you'll notice a lot of overlap. That's a good thing: It means that many of the skills you learn in one segment of the industry can be translated to another.

# 5

# MUSIC PUBLISHING

**W**hile publishing is not often viewed as being the most exciting side of the music industry, it is one of the most important areas and continues to be a healthy and vibrant sector of business. The music publisher's primary job is to ensure that the money that songwriters and composers earn through commercial use of their music is collected on their behalf worldwide.

While certain areas of publishing companies act as accounting firms, there is also a creative side to the company that puts writers together, signs new writers in an A&R capacity and pitches music to film, television and commercials for music licenses and soundtracks. Long after an artist's popular career is over, a smart publishing deal and creative executives have the ability to ensure income streams for many years to come. Every time you hear a song on a TV show, a film or a commercial, a music publisher has negotiated on behalf of that artist to place the music in that location. Music publishers often work closely with record companies in the creative process.

## What Is Music Publishing?

Although publishing is dominated by major companies controlling millions of copyrights, there is a thriving and widely successful class of mid-size publishers, as well as a burgeoning independent publishing scene. To be a publisher you have to have the infrastructure—or a deal with a larger company—to collect on songs in your catalog. You can be a publisher with three songs in your catalog or with 30,000: The process is essentially the same.

Artists choose to do publishing deals for a variety of reasons. For some, early in their career, artists may need money to live on to pursue their artistic endeavors; some may need the A&R and licensing support. Later in artists' careers, they may choose to sell their catalog for long-term financial security. It is not uncommon for superstar artists to fetch hundreds of millions of dollars for a body of work, and in recent years the purchase and sale of artist catalogs has become an exciting business. In many cases, artists' songs continue to go up in value long after they die.

When disputes arise about usage of songs or copyright infringement, the music publisher defends the intellectual property of its writers passionately and effectively. When you hear about legal cases dealing with internet piracy, chances are that there was a music publisher involved in bringing the case to court. With that said, there's a wide spectrum of work within the publishing industry—from legal and accounting to creative and A&R.

Like record labels, publishing companies also have departments that handle the creative, administrative and legal sides of the business, as well as senior management that oversees the entire business.

# Administrative and Legal Jobs

They may not be as glamorous, but the people in administration keep the business moving. A job in the back office can be a good way to learn about the business and to make contacts. Here are a few key players.

### EXECUTIVE ASSISTANT

An executive assistant knows everybody's job and role within the company and represents the executive he/she works for. An executive assitant should be able to delegate calls and tasks to other employees; he/she is responsible for running everything that happens behind the scenes in the office of the executive.

**INSIDE STORY**

**DANNY STRICK**
Co-President
Sony ATV Music
Publishing

*"If you're talking about the creative side of publishing, it's crucial to have an innate ability to know what's commercially viable and what public opinion is. You need the ability to develop relationships with writers and producers so they'll work with you. It's important to create opportunities for your clients by partnering them with other creative people. Developing the trust of the writers is really important. Also, although you don't have to be a musician or know how to write music, you need to relate to writers about their music.*

**Are you ready to...**

■ Manage busy schedules, travel arrangements and executive conversations?

■ Remain confidential with important and private information?

■ Serve as a center of information for your boss, as well as the entire organization?

**You should be...**

■ Aggressive yet respectful, and able to prioritize important calls and meetings.

■ Able to speak for your employer confidently and with accuracy.

■ Trustworthy and able to handle—as well as diffuse—stressful situations.

## ADMINISTRATORS

Publishing company administrators track royalties for the songs in the company's catalog. They produce statements, invoice calculations, statistics sheets, financial reports and more.

**Are you ready to...**

■ Interact with representatives from international markets and interpret monetary transactions?

■ Work with financial models to create reports and statements?

■ Manage large-scale financial accounts?

**You should be...**

- Proficient at math and skilled with accounting.
- Interested in maintaining the financial standing of a major company.
- Able to understand business transactions in a global setting and interpret them for a domestic company.

## LEGAL

Because music publishers deal with copyrights and permissions, their legal departments are especially important. They handle the deals between the writers and publishers and negotiate licenses, acquisitions and partnerships.

**Are you ready to....**

- Negotiate difficult song splits?
- Defend copyrights and intellectual property?

**You should be...**

- Deal-minded and flexible in structuring relationships with creative people.
- Able to seamlessly travel between the corporate boardroom and meetings with songwriters.

# Creative Jobs

Songs—pieces of music of all variety—are the publishing company's stock-in-trade, so the people who find music and pitch it for use by recording artists, TV and film producers, advertisers, etc. are very important. Here are some of the key creative departments at a typical publishing company.

## SYNCHRONIZATION

When a song controlled by a publishing company is used in film or TV, the company grants what's known as a *synchronization license*. This is an important part of the company's revenue stream, and is therefore a key department in the business. People in the synchronization department know their catalog intimately so they're in a position to pitch songs to film, television and commercials based on lyrical themes, music elements, and popular trends.

**You need to...**

■ According to Ron Broitman, Senior Vice President, Head of Synchronization at Warner Chappell Music:

"You should develop a good balance between the creative aspect and the business aspect of music. When listening to music, you have to be able to find that thing that people will love."

**INSIDE STORY**

**RON BROITMAN**
Senior VP, Head of
Synchronization
Warner Chappell Music

*"Being a part of your community and exchanging ideas with your peers are part of the lifestyle of the job. It's not a job, it's a lifestyle—those who treat it as a lifestyle are the people that work longer and have more satisfaction."*

**Are you ready to...**

■ Research media opportunities for music placement in a changing marketplace?

■ Interact with music supervisors, studios, networks and advertising agencies?

■ Pitch and sell music in a competitive marketplace?

■ Negotiate licensing fees based upon market value?

## A&R

Like record labels, publishing companies have artist and repertoire departments that sign songwriters, composers and lyricists (some of whom may be artists in their own right, but not necessarily). You will research charts, attend shows, and locate promising songwriters who can become major players throughout various genres.

**Are you ready to...**

- Go to multiple concerts per night and listen to a lot of demos?
- Spend a lot of time meeting with aspiring artists and writers to develop a wide-reaching network of people who help turn you on to talent?
- Expand songwriters' horizons by creating opportunity in areas that they otherwise may not have been exposed to?

**It helps to...**

- Be aware of the current trends and understand the music marketplace.
- Understand why certain collaborations work better than others.
- Have an ear for potentially successful music.

## HEAD OF CREATIVE

The creative department oversees all signings of new writers, as well as the development of the current roster. The person running this department's job is to manage the creative staff.

## INSIDE STORY

**JAKE OTTMANN**
**Former Vice President**
**of East Coast Creative**
**EMI Music Publishing**

*"My day consists primarily of talking to songwriters. Some are artists (like members of the Fray); some are just pure songwriters who hope to get other artists to sing their material. Good music publishers have to be really organized and keep track of a lot of information. I still take time management classes! You need a highly developed instinct. If you do a lot of research and you're very organized, your instinct is probably going to serve you well."*

**Are you ready to...**

■ Be up to date on the musical landscape—frequently attending concerts to sign new acts?

■ Put artists together with writers and producers?

■ Connect creative people in order to create compatible relationships?

**You should...**

■ Understand trends and styles in the global marketplace.

■ Be able to visualize how specific types of music can function in certain situations.

■ Know every writer of every popular song; be a student of songwriting.

**You should be...**

■ Organized.

■ A good manager.

■ An effective researcher.

# Senior Management

Like record companies, music publishers coordinate all their various departments from the very top.

### CHIEF EXECUTIVE OFFICER
### AND CHIEF FINANCIAL OFFICER

The chief executive officer and chief financial officer oversee all aspects of the publishing company. They are responsible for maintaining the corporate culture and developing a long-term vision. These senior managers oversee all collections, royalties and licensing.

**Are you ready to....**

- Work closely with songwriters?
- Know and understand how song splits and collection fees work?
- Oversee a global licensing marketplace and an international web of collections?

**You should...**

- Possess extensive knowledge of royalty rates and mechanical licensing.
- Have a strong ability to understand music currently and in historical contexts.
- Be creative but also have a strong sense of business and economic factors.
- Have a vision for long-term projects and investment returns.

## Looking Ahead

While the record industry has struggled in recent years, music publishers continue to find creative ways to earn money through licensing music in everything from movies to mobile phones and whatever new platforms emerge. No matter what happens in the future of the music business, it's a good bet that publishers will adapt and persist.

# DISTRIBUTION

**H**istorically, the field of music distribution has been taken for granted. In a system dominated by major labels for the first 40 years, distribution was overlooked by many in the music industry—and almost completely unknown to those looking at the music business from the outside.

But like the man behind the curtain in *The Wizard of Oz,* the people working in distribution were on the side of the business that was crucial, even if it went unnoticed. Managers and artists alike were not exactly aware of how their physical product was making its way into markets, yet distribution served as the key connector between the artist and the fan.

People would not be able to access their favorite artists' work without the distribution industry working to ensure that when music fans went to their local shop, that record was stocked, was marked properly, was priced in a position that it needed to be and was available in the back room if all the copies on the shelf had sold out.

With the change in the industry and the rise of managers, distribution became a topic of increasing interest. In the digital age, the need for distribution actually increased. We now have more artists who don't fit into the major label system but still needed physical product in stores. This led to a strong increase in independent distribution.

## Music Distribution Today

In the digital age, the biggest topic of conversation is whether or not there will be one agreed-upon distribution system for music. How will Spotify, iTunes and similar services affect how music is consumed in the long term? What is the bottom of the physical distribution market, and have we reached that bottom? The configuration of physical product has changed. If you still want a physical CD, you can get it on demand through websites like Amazon; if you don't care about the physical product, you can instantly access music through iTunes or streaming sites.

Distribution companies have become complex entities with experts in digital streaming, digital distribution, marketing, radio promotion, PR and more. These companies have become far more than vehicles for sending out physical product; they have become a support system for individual acts and smaller labels in need of advisement and muscle for areas of the industry far beyond typical distribution needs. We can thank digital distribution for the increase in services provided by these companies.

Have you ever wondered why some albums are more expensive on iTunes than others? Or why only certain songs are available on Spotify? The complexity of distribution decisions revolves around a great amount of market research: It's the job of these companies to decide how much music will sell for, where it will sell and other similar factors.

Simply stated, distribution is the connection between artist and fan. Without it, the most talented artists in the world wouldn't be known outside of their touring circuit. Likewise, the brand new indie band from a small town in the US would have little chance at having their music leave their local scene.

## Jobs in Music Distribution

Music distribution serves as the connector between music and an artist's fan base. As such, a distributor deals with every other sector of the music business to assure effective placement of a product. Here are some of the typical jobs you'll find in music distribution company.

### BUSINESS AND LEGAL AFFAIRS

One of the most important jobs in distribution is getting the product to distribute in the first place. The people in business and legal affairs are in charge of negotiating deals with all of the different record labels. In the areas of physical, mobile and digital distribution, they determine the sales rates.

**Are you ready to...**

- Work closely with smaller labels and imprints to negotiate distribution deals?
- Work closely with international partners to develop worldwide relationships for your entities and labels?
- Actively communicate with the president of the company to develop the partnership philosophy and corporate strategy?

**It helps to...**

- Study all aspects of the distribution model.
- Have a strong knowledge of all aspects of the mass market as it relates to music distribution.
- Understand the most meaningful income streams for individual artists. For example, one artist may do better at digital than at physical.

**In high school you should...**

- Take as many business and law classes as you can to understand negotiations.
- Have a job where you have to negotiate on behalf of musical acts, be it for a venue or a retail store.

## MARKETING

Distribution marketers make sure that the retailers and buyers understand the full scope of the artists and the products they've released, the audience, and the strategy for generating sales. They educate retail outlets on the full story of the artist in order to find the best ways to sell the artists' music.

**Are you ready to...**

- Know a lot about the artists' music and biography that you are distributing?
- Identify and define the selling points in a project?
- Travel extensively to visit retail outlets and spend a lot of time in Minneapolis and Bentonville, Arkansas, the home to major distribution outlets?
- Educate retail stores on the best ways to sell an artist?

**It helps to...**

- Be intrigued by sales and consumer spending habits.
- Have a good understanding of all genres of music.
- Be strong at communicating with executives and business teams, as you will be working closely with a large number of record labels.

**In high school you should...**

- Understand regional music across the country. For example, interpret how bands sound different—and sell differently—based on the region of the country they're from.
- Work with local acts to try to get their music in local record stores.

## ACCOUNTING AND ROYALTIES

As with any business, getting paid is important. With music distribution, this can be very complex, as some of the money com-

### INSIDE STORY

**GARY ARNOLD**
**Former Senior Vice President of Entertainment Marketing**
**Best Buy**

*"Ahmet Ertegun said you have to listen to music with two sets of ears, your own and the public's. At the end of the day, we have to invest our time into things that we think will have commercial opportunities."*

ing in must be redistributed to labels and artists. The accounting and royalty departments must maintain meticulous records of sales, royalties, shipping and returns. You will track all of the company's incoming revenue and outgoing expenses. You will be responsible for generating royalty statements and sending them to all label partners. You will also be expected to collect and collate from international partners and accounts.

**Are you ready to...**
- Calculate royalties owed?
- Work closely with accounts payable and foreign royalty departments to create accurate financial records?

**It helps to be...**
- Math-minded and pay close attention to detail.
- Experienced in accounting.
- Have a strong understanding of and interest in foreign currencies.

**In high school you should...**
- Take as many math and accounting classes as you can.
- Oversee the financial aspects of a school festival, event or club.
- Serve as your high school's treasurer.

## LABEL AND PARTNER RELATIONS

The word "middleman" may seem like a bit of a put-down, but the people who can go in between two separate entities and help them work together play a vital role in all kinds of business. These individuals are especially key in music distribution. They serve as a conduit between the larger distribution entity and the smaller independent label partners for all distribution-related matters, including marketing and manufacturing needs, roster changes and representation within the company.

**Are you ready to...**

- Advocate on behalf of your roster?
- Get to know the music and artistic roster of your label partners even if it isn't the genre or type of bands that you like?
- Manage smaller companies within the confines of your distribution company?

**It helps to...**

- Be a balanced problem solver when it comes to navigating issues and concerns between your employers and your partners.
- Have a good understanding of the issues facing independent record labels.
- Have record label experience to understand distribution needs.

**In high school you should...**

- Take notice of the artists on both major and independent record labels.
- Intern at a record label, start a record label for local bands, or help a local band get signed to a small label.
- Take notice of the challenges that you see facing local

bands in your area as they try to sell music and get signed to record deals.

## ACQUISITIONS

In the distribution field, the people in acquisitions combine research and A&R (see Chapter 4). They spend their time identifying independent labels and acts that have developed a loyal fan base, sales base and following in local geographic areas, and making deals to distribute their music. Because so many artists today release their own music on CD, MP3 or through other means, this job is more challenging—but for many, more interesting—than ever.

**Are you ready to...**

- Listen to a lot of independent music?
- Develop relationships with local record stores nation-wide?
- Examine social media as well as radio reports to tap into new talent?

**It helps to...**

- Develop a good ear and eye for unsigned talent.
- Understand all musical styles and the audiences associated with those styles.
- Be creative-minded but research-oriented.

**In high school you should...**

- Attend a lot of concerts at small venues to discover upcoming talent.

- Use social media sites to learn about new bands and emerging trends.
- Read print and online media covering the latest artists and trends in music.
- Develop relationships with local bands and help them find ways to distribute their music.

## MANUFACTURING

Digital download may have made physical objects like CDs, DVDs, tapes and records less important than they were in the past, but it's still important to offer a version of musical acts in a package that is tangible for certain customers. People in media manufacturing work in major production plants and are responsible for pressing, replicating and shipping physical product to retailers, distributors and labels. Without the manufacturing jobs, no physical music would ever make it to the stores.

**Are you ready to...**

- Work in a factory with pressing machinery?
- Participate in the production of your favorite band's CDs?

**It helps to...**

- Be able to work under specific and important deadlines.
- Be able to effectively multi-task when dealing with many different customers.
- Handle an extremely high volume of product.

**In high school you should...**

- Develop strong organizational skills.
- Take a leadership role in a club to learn how to manage people and priorities.
- Oversee the pressing of some local bands' CDs.

# PRESIDENT

As the president of a distribution company, you oversee the placement of the right amount of music in the right places so that the consumer can find it. You have to make sure that you get the right exposure in the right places. You need a strong understanding of your entire customer base—understand what they want and how they want to buy it.

**Are you ready to...**

- Deal with manufacturing plants to handle orders and shipping?
- Speculate upon the demand of particular artists and interact with buyers of mass retail and independent record stores?
- Deal with online merchants in the sale of digital music product?

**It helps to be...**

- Smart about retail business, with an understanding of consumer buying habits.
- Someone who enjoys spending time in music stores so that you can understand how physical sales operate effectively.

■ Good at forecasting a product's sales potential.

**In high school you should...**

■ Work for or spend time at retail outlets—like Walmart, Best Buy and Target—as well as independent record stores.

■ Work for a company that does sales to learn purchasing, returns and demand. Another good option for learning the sales and distribution process is to work in some capacity within the magazine industry.

## Looking Ahead

Music distribution has changed radically in the last few years, and you can expect it to continue to evolve as more outlets emerge. Some of the traditional ways of selling music may go away—or begin to cater to smaller, more specialized markets—but they'll always be replaced by something new in the popular sphere. It will be the forward-thinking people in distribution who are able to turn "new" into "profitable."

# RECORDING AND PRODUCTION

udio production was once a very specialized profession with clearly defined roles, such as "producer," "audio engineer," "mastering engineer" and so on. Musicians rarely interacted with technology; they wrote, played and sang the songs, while the technicians made the records.

Today, most musicians at least dabble in audio production, thanks to emerging digital technology that allows almost anyone to make multitrack recordings at home. Today, even mobile phones can be used as recording studios!

At the same time, the market for recorded music has evolved and expanded. People involved in audio production still make records; they still capture music and dialog for film and TV and they still work in radio and advertising. The difference now is that they may also be creating ring tones for phones, sample libraries for digital instruments and audio for video games.

## The Studio Comes Home

From the '50s to the early '90s, almost all production was done in professional studios. These facilities would have a staff of engineers, assistants, technicians and support personnel, with finely tuned rooms designed to attract producers. These studios covered the gamut, from world-class facilities used by the stars to small demo studios used by lesser-known clients.

Today, most of the lower-end facilities have been replaced by home studios or project studios run by an owner-operator (which may well be a home studio with slightly better equipment). The good side of this transition is that you can learn to record at home; the bad news is that the mentoring and apprenticeship once available through starting in a small job at a studio is becoming less and less available.

What makes a great producer? That is the million dollar question, and often times everyone has a different answer. There are essentially two paths within the production world: there is the self-taught, homemade approach and the more traditional, educated approach. There are pros and cons to each, and finding your niche within production doesn't mean that you'll have to choose one camp over the other.

The homemade approach has proliferated over the past 10

years because of how inexpensive technology has become. The self-taught producer has become increasingly common; rather than using traditional sounds and methods, they rely heavily on intuition, feel and their artistic vision. In a sense, they are free to do whatever they want. They are not restricted by conventions and can create something very innovative and different.

Production has become much more democratic because of this accessibility to technology, and with that comes two opposing realities. First, the industry can now discover hidden gems—innovative producers who, in an earlier time, would not have had access to production equipment. Conversely, this accessibility floods the musical landscape and there is a lot of poor production that would not have seen the light of day before advanced technology became easily accessible.

The second approach has one foot in the traditional world of production and one in the contemporary world. Generally, people in this category are more experienced in traditional education. This does not necessarily mean they were educated in academic programs, but perhaps through internships, apprenticeships or combinations of all of these. Because they develop a strong understanding of the details and methods of production, these are generally people who are more versatile and can go from artist to artist or genre to genre without much problem. They are also better prepared to deal with issues that may arise during the production process.

It's essential for those in either category of the production world to keep their egos in check. Though producers bring a strong artistic vision to the project, the final product is about the artist, and all of the choices need to be made in order to support and serve the artist.

To work in audio production, you must also be extremely detail-oriented: A producer oversees both the technical and creative aspects of a recording. You have to know where every-thing—and everyone—is at any given moment. In the digital age, it can often be hard to keep track of everything. If you lose the masters on a hard drive in a different area of town, you're going to be held responsible for the consequences. This intense responsibility is not all bad though: With it comes the ability to both express your creative vision and to facilitate an artist's transition from dreams to reality.

## Jobs in Audio Recording

Aside from the support staff that might work in a big stu-dio—people like the studio manager, receptionist, etc., who rarely take part in the recording sessions themselves—audio production is a field with a lot of overlap. Not all producers are technically proficient engineers, but most at least know the basics. Not all engineers are good players or arrangers, but they should have an understanding of music and a solid knowledge of how instruments sound. Some people special-ize in a style or genre—such as classical, jazz, R&B, etc. Oth-ers work with a range of different artists.

### PRODUCER

In audio, the word "producer" can have many meanings. Some producers are known for creating a sonic signature, like Phil Spector's famous "Wall of Sound." Others are known for helping artists to maximize their own unique talents.

Some producers rarely touch the equipment; others take care of every detail, from microphone placement to mixing. In dance music, producers are often people working on their own (or in teams) to produce backing tracks, one reason why many R&B and pop albums will feature several different producers, each responsible for one or more track.

Some stars have also been great producers for other artists: Phil Collins, David Bowie, Electric Light Orchestra's Jeff Lynn, One Republic's Ryan Tedder and Timbaland are just a few examples. Other great producers are virtually unknown outside of the industry. You may never have heard of Phil Ramone, but I'll bet you know some of the artists he's worked with: Billy Joel, B.B. King, Paul Simon and many others. George Martin produced mainly comedy at EMI records before he met the Beatles, but his knowledge of music theory and arranging and sound proved to be a perfect match for the Fab Four's natural songwriting ability, and together, they produced the most influential music ever made.

## INSIDE STORY

**NICK SANSANO**
Producer

*"The producer needs to recognize that it's the artist's record; it's about the album or the song. It's all fun and games until something messes up, because then it's your fault—even if it isn't your fault."*

No matter what kind of producer you become, you have to be an artist at heart. You should constantly be trying to make the best music possible in an organized and effective fashion. Producers help shape songs, albums and arrangements into a viable commercial package. They help artists articulate the vision of their music and turn it into a finished recording. Producers oversee all aspects of a recording: technical, artistic, business and human resources. A producer must have the ability to hear a raw demo of a song and know what sounds and parts will work best for it. They should also know which side musicians and engineers to use on a particular track, and understand what equipment will bring the best results.

Good producers are also part psychologist and diplomat; they must know how to encourage an artist when things aren't working, and how to guide them towards good creative decisions. Producers sometimes have to smooth things over between artists and their labels, and even between band members! When things go wrong, they often take the heat. But when things go right, they are in demand, sometimes juggling multiple projects at the same time.

### INSIDE STORY

**JIM ANDERSON**
**GRAMMY Award-**
**Winning Engineer**

*What elements are key? "You can have the best engineering skills in the world but if you're not a people person, forget it. Frankly those interpersonal skills are more important than your engineering chops. In addition, you should be as good a musician as you possibly can. You want to become an expert in whatever style you're working in. It's very difficult to cross genres: you can't be all things to all people. You want to look at longevity. If you're just looking at flavor of the month, you're looking at a pretty short career."*

### Are you ready to...

■ Work closely with artists, songwriters, arrangers and musicians?

■ Comfortably insert your creative opinions and abilities into the writing and arranging of the music?

■ Manage a budget? Manage personnel: the band, the record executives, the musicians, the studio managers?

■ Make technical decisions regarding

studio, recording platforms and mastering platforms?

■ Make the artist's record, not yours? Interpret the artist's vision, not your own?

**It helps to be...**

■ In control of your ego.

■ Easy going and open-minded.

■ Aware of both music and the technology used to record it.

■ Comfortable communicating with both creative and business-minded people.

■ Aware of contracts and negotiation skills.

**In high school you can...**

■ Learn about music history and listen to a lot of older records, as well as new releases.

■ Take music technology classes for different software platforms.

■ Learn the basics of music theory, arranging and orchestration.

■ Study communication and psychology.

## RECORDING ENGINEER

An engineer handles the actual details of recording musical performances. This is the person responsible for setting up the microphones, running them into the recorder, adjusting the sound equipment, running the recorder and keeping track of all of the material captured.

First and foremost, engineers need to understand how

their equipment works. For example, they must know which kinds of microphones work best with which instruments and situations, where to position the mics, how to set the levels of the audio equipment between the mic and the recorder, etc. They must have a solid understanding of electronic signal processing, digital recording and mixing technology and the physics of music.

Engineers should also know about the latest audio effects and be able to identify the technical aspects of sound just by listening, the same way a musician should be able to hear the difference between a saxophone and a trumpet. Anyone can turn up the treble on an equalizer, but an engineer should know why that may or may not be a good move.

Ultimately, engineers have a very profound responsibility: to capture that special performance. Nothing is more heartbreaking than playing the perfect take only to listen back and discover that there's unwanted noise or distortion on the track, or that the ending was cut off, or that the drums sound hollow because a mic wasn't set up correctly.

In addition to capturing a performance, engineers also set the balance and often mix the tracks. In fact, some engineers specialize in mixing as opposed to tracking.

Although engineering can be creative in its own right, and although many of the best engineers have a knack for creating sounds no one's ever heard before, this job usually involves less intense collaboration with the artists.

This means that engineers often get to work on a more diverse array of projects than producers. The same technical knowledge they might use to record a hip-hop track also applies to soundtracks, hard rock, folk or country music. That said, some engineers do prefer to specialize in genres, and many develop long-term partnerships with producers and artists.

Engineering is a career in itself, but it can also be a skill that musicians, songwriters and producers develop and apply as a "day job" to help expand their ability to earn income in-between their personal creative projects. Engineers can be part of a production company or recording studio, or they may be independent freelancers who work on projects as they come their way.

**Are you ready to...**

- Spend long hours in the studio?
- Do highly detailed technological work?
- Experiment with sounds?
- Study all the latest technologies and be ahead of the technological curve?

**It helps to be...**

- Detail-oriented and patient.
- A good listener.
- Adept at recognizing the right equipment needed to achieve a specific sound.
- Capable of applying a solid understanding of the physics of sound.

**In high school you should...**

- Take computer science and physics classes.
- Record your own or your friends' music.

- Protect your hearing: Don't use ear buds!
- Work on school productions, live sound reinforcements.
- Be the AV person mixing for media projects.

## MIXING ENGINEER

Mixing is the art of combining all of the individual tracks in a multitrack recording and blending them into a cohesive final product. The mixer's job is to give the recording a personality—to make it sonically and commercially relevant within the artist's chosen genre. Producers and recording engineers also spend time mixing, but some people specialize in what many consider to be an art in its own right.

Most of the same skills that apply to engineering in general apply here, though mixers rarely have to set up mics or record tracks. With today's digital technology, the act of mixing can involve a lot more than setting the relative loudness of various tracks. Mixers will edit audio, sometimes move parts in and out, choose which tracks are heard and which are muted, and even manipulate the audio in creative ways. Most mixes are refined through many different passes, then edited using automation until every setting is ideal. Then they are "printed" or "bounced" into a finished master.

Live sound (or sound reinforcement) mixers do much the same thing as recording mixers, but instead of blending tracks, they blend live musicians (sometimes along with prerecorded material). Sound mixers also work in the film industry and radio, and while each of these fields has specific variations, the basic job is very similar.

**Are you ready to...**

- Spend long hours working individually?
- Research sonic trends? Not just casually listen to music: Treat it as research and listen to it critically to understand the trends?
- Learn how to apply audio processing to individual tracks to help them blend?
- Understand the creative use of audio effects?
- Take detailed criticism?
- Listen to music constantly?

**You should be...**

- Up to date on all of the current production trends and recording and editing platforms.
- Able to recognize minute sonic details.
- Able to form strong relationships with bands, producers, artist managers and A&R reps.

**In high school you can...**

- Pay attention to the records that you like and find out who mixed them, along with popular songs you hear on the radio.
- Experiment with mixing software on your home computer.
- Try to mirror or mimic existing styles in addition to creating your own style. Experiment with different styles and sounds.
- Intern or shadow with a mixer in your area or mix local acts for free.

## MASTERING ENGINEER

Mastering is the last stage of the recording process before manufacturing and distribution. Once a mix is finished, the track, called a "master," is given to a final engineer for preparation. Unlike a mixer, the mastering engineer does not generally work on the multitrack, but on the stereo (or surround sound) version of each song.

Mastering engineers also sequence the album—set the transitions between songs. Their job is to make sure that the overall balance is correct in each song (for example, making sure there's not too much bass, or that the most intense sections aren't too loud compared to the quietest), and that the audio tone on all of an album's tracks blend together to create a cohesive unit—even if the tracks were engineered and mixed by different people. A mastering engineer then prepares albums for commercial release in consumer playback systems, film, TV and radio broadcast.

**Are you ready to...**

- Work individually in a detail-oriented atmosphere?
- Make critical technical decisions?
- Recognize the smallest, most minute sounds in a recording?

**You need to be...**

- A listener with strong analytical skills.
- Comfortable with recording and editing software.
- Ready to design your own work environment and your own system.

- Conscious of design and acoustics and comfortable with audio conversions.

**In high school you can...**
- Read and understand all of the different elements of engineering a record.
- Develop a strong knowledge of all methods of recording.
- Listen to good audio recordings and experiment with equalizers and compressors to "remaster" them for your own audio system.

## ASSISTANT ENGINEER

The primary role of the assistant engineer is to help the tracking or mixing engineer. Assistants are often newer at the business, and while the money's not great, part of the "pay" is getting to learn the trade from a more seasoned pro. When an outside engineer comes to the studio, a staff assistant is often assigned to make sure that they have everything they need. Therefore, the assistant should know the ins and outs of all of the equipment and the studio wiring.

**Are you ready to...**
- Set up microphones, patch the outboard gear to running data backups and keep documentation?
- Serve as a crucial set of eyes, ears, hands and feet for the engineer?
- Be called upon to take on roles on the upper and lower margins of the job—at some points filling in for the

engineer, at others taking lunch orders or making coffee?

**It helps to be...**

- Able to pay close attention to the flow of a session for extended hours on very little sleep.
- Extremely diplomatic: know how to choose your words carefully and communicate clearly.
- Able to learn the minute details of the studio so that everyone has complete confidence in your technical skills.

**In high school you can...**

- Learn as much about recording as possible.
- Read audio and trade magazines to familiarize yourself with current practices and technology.
- Help record local bands at a studio.
- Volunteer to assist at a local studio (or even a local home recording setup).
- Join your school's recording club.

## REMIXING ENGINEER/PRODUCER

Remixing isn't as purely technical as it sounds. Remixing doesn't simply mean resetting the balance on an existing mix: It can often mean creating a completely new backing track and arrangement of a song, usually for a dance audience. Often times DJs, artists or producers will take an existing track and add musical elements that change the sound and aesthetic of the original—whether it's changing a pop song into a dance track or a rock song into a hip-hop track.

Thanks to the popularity of dance music, remixing has become a very lucrative area of the business.

**Are you ready to...**

- Experiment with music software?
- Understand a wide variety of musical genres and recognize the various sonic details that are relevant for each?
- Put your own stamp on songs from different artists?
- Learn how to program sounds with synthesizers and drum machines?
- Apply audio effects in a creative way?

**You need to...**

- Understand digital audio editing and mixing.
- Have a strong sense of what musical elements combine well.
- Be able to bring original sounds to existing songs.

**In high school you can...**

- Look at web tutorials on remixing to hone your skills.
- Create your own remixes.
- Establish an online presence for your remixes on a YouTube channel, blog and/or website.

## EQUIPMENT TECHNICIAN

The equipment technician (or "tech") oversees the technical well-being of a studio. This includes repair and preventative maintenance for a wide array of equipment, which may include analog and digital devices, computers, tape machines, microphones and the wiring that connects all of the equipment. The technician may also make recommendations for equipment purchases and technical practices to be utilized by the engineering staff.

**Are you ready to...**

- Troubleshoot and repair complex equipment that is malfunctioning?
- Evaluate what studio equipment is needed?

**You should...**

- Have good problem solving skills, be able to think clearly under pressure, be able to find creative solutions to sticky problems and be able to recognize when to move on from ideas that are not working.
- Be patient and have a natural curiosity as to how things work.
- Be able to think through complex issues with great attention to detail.

## SOUND DESIGNER

Like a remixer, a sound designer combines creative and technical skills. The job is to create unique sounds, usually with electronic equipment such as synthesizers and samplers. The main markets for sound design are film (audio effects) and the musical instrument industry (creating preset sounds for synthesizers, sample libraries and audio effects).

Some sound designers also do traditional recording. For example, creating an orchestral sound library will involve recording violins, cellos, etc. These recordings can then be manipulated to sound either natural or completely new. While many sound designers are employed by companies to work behind the scenes, some develop a name for themselves with signature libraries of their own, designed to expand the capability of music software and hardware.

**Are you ready to...**

- Master the controls of synthesizers and effects?
- Use audio editing software in creative ways?
- Work with equipment makers to understand the details of their products and apply those to creating sounds?

**You should...**

- Understand audio synthesis and signal processing.
- Know how to edit sounds with digital audio software.

**In high school you can...**

- Study the principles of analog synthesis.
- Experiment with the controls of software or hardware instruments.
- Experiment by combining unusual sounds and applying audio effects to them.

## STUDIO MANAGER/OWNER

The studio manager/owner oversees the entire studio operation, from the minor details to the major decisions. Of course, some studios are owned by producers, engineers or artists, but unless they're just starting out, they'll likely need someone to handle day-to-day business so they can focus on making recordings.

The manager is responsible for a variety of jobs. He/she organizes the booking calendar, bills the clients, pays the staff and sets the budget for equipment purchase and maintenance. A studio manager hires employees (full time, freelance or both) and oversees security, all the while making sure that coffee is always flowing and snacks are always available to keep a session running. The stuio manager keeps clients happy.

Managers don't need any studio skills at all, but they should have enough people skills to develop a solid network of both clients (artists, producers, record labels) and service providers (recording engineers, techs, session musicians, etc.). A basic understanding of marketing—important to keep the business coming in—doesn't hurt either.

### Are you ready to...

- Hire and train staff to make sure that the studio operates smoothly?
- Keep the studio busy with clients?
- Oversee all major decisions about equipment purchases?

### It helps to have...

- Excellent interpersonal and networking skills for both attracting clients and managing employees.
- A good head for business, numbers and money.

■ The ability to manage crises and think clearly under pressure.

**In high school you can...**

■ Learn as much as possible about running a small business and balancing books.

■ Learn about recording technology, both in terms of understanding the needs of clients and in terms of purchasing equipment. New equipment is an investment that should be made wisely, considering both vintage gear as well as current and future technologies.

# Looking Ahead

The recording business has changed radically in the last 20 years. It was once a more structured profession than it is today. In some ways, this makes it harder to find a clear career path.

On the other hand, opportunities now exist that weren't even conceived of 20 years ago—things like ringtones, video games, mobile apps and sample libraries provide work for producers and engineers today that never existed before. Technology continues to bring many more new and as yet unimagined opportunities.

Recognizing this trend, colleges, universities and community colleges have greatly expanded the number of courses that teach all aspects of audio production, from engineering to sound design and production. It's become part of many musicians' education as well as a major in its own right.

The legitimacy of and possibilities in the recorded music

industry continue to expand with emerging technology and appreciation for music as an academic pursuit. Production is key to assuring quality and harnessing creativity in the music workspace, and will continue to thrive alongside technological advances.

# MEDIA

**M**usic and media have gone hand-in-hand for centuries, from the use of instruments to send military signals to the chiming of clocks to tell townspeople the time.

Today, the relationship works two ways. First, music is used in, and is part of, various media. Turn on the news, and the first thing you hear is a theme song. Even talk radio is filled with music. The Internet allows music to be used in an even greater variety of ways. Even text-heavy blogs will often have a jukebox providing music as you read.

Second, the media is used to promote and comment on music. From outlets like newspapers, magazines, TV shows and radio to media like blogs, webcasts, podcasts and the like, there's an almost overwhelming number of avenues for people to communicate about music.

## Understanding the Media

You can look at the media from two different perspectives. If you're a musician or record executive, you'll want to develop a solid understanding and a good working relationship with every form of media you can. Media is the manner of which you communicate with fans and the public at large. Using messages you control, as well as messages you don't control, you have to engage in a complex web of players where the decisions you make—and the manner in which you decide to express yourself—will directly affect the number of people you reach, how you reach them and what impression you leave when you do.

The other perspective is that of a critic who provides commentary on music in one form or another. This is the one of the most interesting sectors of the industry because it has a constantly evolving relationship with music. It's well suited for individuals who are interested in trying new things through technology. There are many different audiences and each has its own set of criteria. For example, some media members offer expert advice, instruction or reviews to other musicians. They may write about gear, or conduct interviews with professionals about their craft. These media members may be musicians, producers or executives themselves.

Other media members write for a "consumer" audience. Some may have great taste and the ability to communicate about what makes a particular artist, song or album worth checking out. Others may not really know that much about music, but may have a knack for conducting interviews that deliver the kinds of personal stories that fans seem to love. Yet others may have a great nose for news, reporting on new trends before anyone else knows they even exist. Some are great at analyzing business trends and explaining where the money is going.

The opportunities in media are virtually endless: If you enjoy doing creative work interacting with technology, and explaining things to people, it's the perfect area for you. There are jobs for the artistically inclined, the verbally inclined and everyone in between. From the printed word to the digital space, there are many different avenues of expression and communication. To be successful requires a good understanding of how to use these various avenues.

## Getting Started

As with the music industry, the media's gatekeepers—i.e., editors and publishers—no longer have a monopoly on deciding who can distribute their work. The digital age has allowed people to begin careers in the media industry from increasingly young ages. People are able to express themselves and market others—whether using blogs, social media sites or other means. You no longer have to wait until you have a college degree hanging on your wall to begin your career.

Being a student in high school and college is a great time to start putting your creative skills to work by covering local concerts, readings or other cultural events. As Maura Johnston, music editor of the Village Voice, explained in an interview, "Curiosity is really key." If you apply your various interests and curiosities to explaining and writing about the world around you, you're already heading in the right direction.

Jobs in the media can be high profile or relatively anonymous. Some opt to be a name in print or a face on the screen; others prefer to be the editor who gives the high-profile writer's work some shape, or the producer, director or camera person behind the scenes. There are jobs for the technically minded—lighting, crew, audio recording, audio and video editing—and for the literary minded. The media provides jobs for photographers, cinematographers and graphic designers (for print, the web and, increasingly, mobile apps), and animators. There are opportunities for people who can create the programs and apps that have become important media outlets. There are even jobs for those who don't aspire to create the content, but instead have a knack for sales, marketing, distribution and management.

You can juggle multiple assignments at once and—once you've become successful—you can pick and choose projects of interest. In a given week, you can cover an up-and-coming band at your favorite music venue, talk on a podcast about upcoming album releases, write a piece about trends in contemporary hip-hop and help edit articles that are ready to go to print.

With all this opportunity, the media industry is ideal for self-starters—those who are able to come up with several ideas and run with them, meeting deadlines all the while.

While an Internet connection is all you need to get started on your own, media as a whole is a collaborative enterprise. Whether it is editors working with journalists or creative directors working with photographers, the collaboration between creative minds in the media sector ensures that the final product communicates its message clearly and effectively. So, if you're interested in communicating your artistic vision or opinions to the public in some form—be it photography, logo design or anything else—this may be the place for you. Here are some of the basic jobs in media. Note, however, that these continue to change and overlap.

# Journalist

The Mirriam-Webster dictionary defines a journalist as "an editor of or writer for a newspaper or magazine or radio and television news." If that seems to cover a lot of ground, well, there's a reason for that: Journalism is a profession with many definitions.

A news reporter who concerns herself with the facts is a journalist; so is a columnist or critic who spouts opinions. Journalists can write short pieces (like mini reviews), longer feature articles or whole books. They can produce 60-second news reports or movie-length documentaries. They can use print, the Internet, radio, TV and more.

### JOURNALISM JOBS

Being a journalist can consist of anything from covering concerts, conducting interviews with artists, reviewing new album releases and/or reporting on music news. Here are a few of the categories within the wider field of journalist.

- ■ **REPORTER**: Seeks information and provides it in a timely and accurate fashion.
- ■ **COLUMNIST**: Offers opinion, usually based on a current new topic and within a specific regular format (i.e. a weekly single page story, a daily radio spot, a nightly TV spot).
- ■ **FEATURE WRITER**: Writes long form articles, which may be interviews with individuals or longer reports using a variety of sources, or some combination of the formats above.
- ■ **MUSIC/FILM/BOOK/DRAMA CRITIC**: In print, online, radio or TV offers opinion about current media.
- ■ **PRODUCT REVIEWER**: Assesses and explains the latest equipment. One branch of this area of journalism focuses more on the gear designed to create music (instruments, equipment, software, etc.); another focuses on products used to listen to music (music players, headphones, etc.).
- ■ **"HOW-TO" EXPERT**: The media is a powerful teaching tool, and experts can explain everything from how to tune a guitar to how to write a filmscore or run a record label.

Many journalists find themselves in many of the above roles at various times in their careers. While the specifics may change, the essence of the job is the same: You want to learn the facts and explain them as clearly as possible in a way that's relevant to your audience.

**Are you ready to...**

- Research potential stories and summarize them in a clear form?
- Conduct interviews that uncover new information?
- Understand the audience and tailor the story to their interests?
- Take direction on a story to make it appropriate for the media outlet in question?
- Juggle multiple writing projects and work under tight deadlines?
- Pitch your story ideas to editors and producers?
- Work on a freelance basis?
- See a story through necessary revisions?

**It helps to...**

- Have the ability to write clearly and concisely.
- Develop strong research skills.
- Cultivate a willingness to ask unexpected (and sometimes unwelcome) questions.
- Have strong time management skills.
- Be self-motivated and conscious of deadlines.
- Have the ability to make and maintain contacts, build relationships and develop a network of sources.
- Dedicate time to the discipline to documenting your work and supporting your conclusions.

**In high school you can...**

- Start your own music blog.
- Write for or edit your school newspaper.

■ Intern at your local newspaper, cable TV outlet or radio station.

■ Work in your school's radio or AV departments.

## EDITOR

Editors can have many roles, but most fall into one of the following categories:

■ **COPY EDITORS**: Correct text for grammar, spelling and word flow. Proofreaders fall under this category, though their job is very specifically to look for both text and graphical mistakes and to make sure that every story meets the publications style and print guidelines.

■ **MANAGING EDITORS**: Manage the flow of copy between the writers, other editors, designers and production department.

■ **ASSIGNING EDITORS** (sometimes ranked as associate, senior, executive or department editors, such as "reviews editor," "gear editor," "fim editor" etc.): Choose topics and assign writers to stories, oversee their completion and make sure the stories meet the publication's needs. Many of these editors also write quite often.

■ **EDITOR-IN-CHIEF**: Oversees an entire publication, chooses stories, works with designers to create each issue.

■ **ASSISTANT EDITOR**: an entry-level position working under one of the above editors. Assistant editors may do some writing or even be assigned small pieces.

No matter which category of editorial job you're in, working as an editor at a music publication, you will read countless articles and prepare them for publication. This includes—but isn't limited to—proofreading for technical mistakes like grammar and spelling, as well as mistakes in content like facts, dates and statistics. The job isn't just proofreading though: you'll also have responsibilities like developing story ideas to assign to writers.

**Are you ready to...**

- Develop and assign story ideas?
- Edit articles to prepare them for publication?
- Work with the art department to make sure the articles are formatted correctly for the publication?

**You should...**

- Have a strong attention to detail and a mastery of journalistic prose style.
- Be able to work well in a collaborative environment.
- Pay close attention to all major music outlets to know the current landscape of music news.

**In high school you can...**

- Serve as the editor of your school newspaper.
- Take journalism, creative writing and English classes.
- Start a music blog with friends and edit their submissions in addition to writing your own.

---

### INSIDE STORY

**MAURA JOHNSTON**
**Former Music Editor**
**Village Voice**

*"You need confidence. Have faith in your opinions and the work you're doing. Faith that maybe you don't know everything but you want to learn. I also think curiosity is really key and it helps scuttle a lot of the problems. The closer you can get to the truth about what you're writing about, the better your writing will be."*

# Graphic and Visual Arts

Almost every form of media today includes some kind of graphical treatment, whether it's the typography used to create headlines to the photography and illustrations used to illustrate stories.

Skills in graphics can be put to use in a number of different ways and arenas. Journalistic media outlets need graphic design, but so do record labels, media production companies and even artists themselves. Here are a few key positions.

## GRAHPIC DESIGNER

Graphic designers, managed by a head designer known as a creative director, develop the vision for the brand of their client in all forms of media, including logo, video and website—everything the public is going to see and interact with. They also develop the strategy of how such a brand amplifies and connects with the reader. (As you may recall, record labels use graphic designers to create their packaging, logos, etc. Artists and managers may also use graphic designers to create posters, logos, and the like).

Graphic designers can be highly trained and there are many different jobs within the discipline. Today, almost all graphic design is done with software.

**Are you ready to...**
- Think strategically and creatively simultaneously?
- Present your ideas with confidence and trust in your vision?
- Fully immerse yourself in your brand and your client?

- Use visual ideas to enhance text?
- Choose and prepare photographs for print?
- Use typography?
- Format text to fit into specific page sizes and other spaces?

**It helps to be...**

- Artistically and culturally aware.
- Observant and able to draw inspiration from diverse sources.
- Good at researching photographs.
- Well-organized.
- Able to keep track of both text and visual material from a range of sources.
- Able to collaborate with editors/producers to meet their goals.

**In high school you can...**

- Read magazines and pay attention to logos and advertisements.
- Embrace and believe in your passion.
- Take classes in graphic design.
- Work on your school's yearbook, newspaper or other publications.
- Be aware of current events beyond your core interests, both visually and beyond.
- Understand how global communities and artists are positioning themselves and how this changes in different parts of the world.

## PHOTOGRAPHER

Photographers document, chronicle, cover and memorialize live music events and appearances, and create publicity materials. A photographer might shoot a rock star onstage one day, work on a studio photoshoot another and shoot some products for a how-to article or review on a third.

Music photography is an artform in itself, and the work of top photographers has withstood the test of time. Many have become famous in their own right for their contribution to the entertainment world.

While some publications do have staff photographers, most work as freelancers, often through an agency. The best way to get work is to take pictures and to create a portfolio showing your capabilities.

**Are you ready to...**

- Attend a lot of concerts and be in the front row snapping photos?
- Spend long hours doing photo shoots and editing images?
- Continually educate yourself on new techniques, technologies and methodologies?
- Invest money in new equipment and facilities?

**It helps to be...**

- Passionate about the art of photography.
- Proficient in Adobe Photoshop and other software editing tools.
- Knowledgeable about how to run and maintain

your own business.

■ Strong at networking and promoting yourself professionally.

### In high school you can...

■ Study photography.

■ Take photos for your school newspaper.

■ Take photos covering live concerts and events.

■ Take courses on various editing programs.

■ Create a photo website, including any/all photos to establish your brand (they do not all have to be music-based).

## PHOTO EDITOR

A photo editor researches and chooses images for a publication. The job involves both research and artistic judgment. In this field, an understanding of music history (pop and otherwise) is helpful.

### Are you ready to...

■ Develop contacts with photographers and photo agencies?

■ Research and choose images to go with a story?

### It helps to be...

■ Well-versed in photographic publications and photographers.

■ Organized.

■ Knowledgeable about musicians and musical eras.

**In high school you can...**

- Work for your school newspaper and/or yearbook.
- Take courses on various editing programs.
- Intern at a local newspaper or magazine.
- Create your own website to curate images.

## ILLUSTRATOR

Illustrators design artwork for websites, album covers, concert programs, logos, graphic design, merchandise, and publications. Some of the work can be purely creative. Other times, illustration involves technical drawing.

**Are you ready to...**

- Brainstorm with a marketing or editorial team to decide on a visual direction?
- Express ideas and messages through your drawings or other graphical techniques?
- Make revisions to meet editorial or marketing requirements?

**It helps to be...**

- Creative and curious about art, illustration and design.
- Knowledgeable about art, music and the ways in which they compliment each other.
- A good communicator who both enjoys working in a collaborative environment and takes feedback well.
- Well-versed in software like Adobe Illustrator and Photoshop.
- Knowledgeable in the basics of graphic design.

**In high school you can...**

- Draw for your school newspaper or yearbook.
- Study art.
- Study graphic design.
- Learn design software.
- Offer to design school swag to be sold at sporting events and concerts.
- Create logos for local businesses.

## STYLIST

A stylist helps a photo subject (for example, a musical artist) establish their visual image and ensure that their look remains updated, creative and not trendy, but timeless.

**Are you ready to...**

- Scour shops and websites for the perfect clothes, shoes and accessories?
- Determine a look and feel that best represents the artist in various situations?
- Build professional relationships with hair and color stylists, fashion designers, boutiques, etc., and match them with the artist?

**It helps to be...**

- Fashion forward and stylish.
- Passionate about the world of fashion.
- Knowledgeable about body types/personalities and what compliments and enhances both.

**In high school you can...**

■ Take design and sewing classes.

■ Offer to shop for and dress your friends.

■ Work in a boutique/clothing store.

## PUBLISHER

A publisher oversees the business of a publication whether it be print or digital. Publishers are also responsible for the industry side of the endeavor—marketing, advertising and sales, partnerships and branding.

**Are you ready to...**

■ Create and manage the content of the publication?

■ Hire editors, designers, ad sales people and other key personnel?

■ Set and manage a publication's budget?

■ Look for ways to increase revenue through distribution and advertising sales?

**It helps to be...**

■ Organized with a knack for managing people and multiple projects at the same time.

■ Good at prioritizing and making big decisions.

**In high school you can...**

■ Start your own blog or fanzine.

■ Write and/or take a leadership role in your student newspaper.

■ Work at a local newspaper.

# "New" Media

The internet has greatly expanded the definition of "media" to include outlets that simply didn't exist a few years ago— from YouTube to the blogesphere to whatever new channels that will come along to share ideas with a potential audience. Here are a few current categories within the new media.

## PODCASTER

Podcasters are tastemakers responsible for investigating and reporting on news, current affairs and interesting information. They also host interviews and introduce the public to new ideas, artists, brands and companies.

**Are you ready to...**

- Find and/or generate ideas for stories/features and then pitch them to air?
- Identify interesting guests for interviews?
- Develop and maintain contacts and relationships?
- Record and edit audio (and/or video) and prepare it for online publication?
- Distribute your podcast through iTunes or other outlets?

**It helps to be...**

- Outgoing and comfortable when speaking on microphone (or camera) to large groups of people.
- A good listener who makes people feel comfortable and confident.
- "In the know" on what's current, happening and hot at the time.

- Technically savvy enough to produce and prepare each episode of your podcast.
- Disciplined and organized enough to produce a regular cast, often with only your own deadlines to drive you.

**In high school you can...**

- Start your own podcast or web series.
- Join a student group for public speaking and/or debate.
- Interview friends or local celebrities.

## BLOGGER

You can think of bloggers as independent journalists, or as people who just want a forum to offer their own opinions. Either way, blogging is a great way to get into journalism because it gives you what every person needs the most: experience.

It's easy to set up your own blog, though some people contribute to nationally known blogs instead of (or in addition to) writing for their own. Blogs can include text, photos, audio, video or all of the above.

**Are you ready to...**

- Develop your own unique voice and outlook?
- Design a strategy to attract and build your fan base?
- Develop and maintain contacts and relationships?

**It helps to be...**

- Dedicated to the craft of writing and mastering your own voice.

■ Willing to share a lot of yourself, including your beliefs and ideas.

■ Observant, with a distinct point of view.

**In high school you can...**

■ Start your own blog.

■ Take writing classes.

■ Study digital photography, audio and video production.

■ Learn basic HTML coding.

## SOCIAL MEDIA MARKETING

Social media has provided more ways than ever to interact with fans, and outlets like Facebook and Twitter have become central to promoting and marketing an artist. Unlike any other jobs, this is an area of uncharted territory where the rules can be made as you go along—there's a ton of room for innovation and new ideas.

**Are you ready to...**

■ Blend technology, publicity and marketing?

■ Use social media sites to interact with fans?

**It helps to be...**

■ Strategic. Like a good chess player, you need to know when to make certain moves.

■ Tech savvy but also able to interact with people on a personal basis.

■ Able to envision a long-term strategy that communicates the artists' ideas in the language of the fan.

**In high school you can…**

- Help local bands establish fan bases through social media outlets.
- Volunteer to help run the social media of a small business to attract new customers.
- Get involved with new social media sites to see how they work—make yourself an expert on all of the different sites.

## MANAGING FAN CLUBS AND "PREMIUM" PACKAGES

This job centers around demonstrating an artist's appreciation for his/her fan base via exclusive offerings and premium positioning on tickets. The function of fan clubs is to generate loyalty by using exclusivity to create added value. Fan clubs give acces to many things—bundled packages, special access and everything in between.

**Are you ready to…**

- Work closely with zealous throngs of fans?
- Design and create original and exclusive content to offer fans?
- Use this platform as a means of generating income while not making fans feel like they're being taken advantage of?

**It helps to be…**

- A fan of the artist that you're working with, able to relate to your customers.
- Able to walk the line between serving the needs of the

fan and the needs of the artist.

■ Ready to determine when you're over-servicing and when you're under-servicing and react accordingly.

**In high school you can...**

■ Join a number of fan clubs to understand how certain artists provide services to their fans.

■ Serve as a local representative for larger bands.

■ Organize your own fan clubs for bands that you love.

# Audio and Video

Audio and video production remain important parts of traditional media, but thanks to inexpensive equipment and editing tools, they're also increasingly important in new and independent media.

On the audio side, many of the same kinds of jobs and skills we covered in Chapter 7—recording, mixing and editing audio to prepare it for distribution—apply here. Only in this case, the distribution may be over the airwaves ot streaming online instead of in the form of CD or MP3 album releases. Here are a few other key audio/video jobs related to music media.

## VIDEO PRODUCER

A video producer is responsible for taking all the moving parts of a production and managing them from inception to delivery. A producer serves as a liaison between various creative parties to ensure that everyone is satisfied with the end product. He/she makes sure all equipment is in place (and that the right people are on hand to run it), manages the budget and more.

**Are you ready to...**
- Be responsible for all aspects of the shoot including creative, financial and administrative?
- Settle creative disputes?
- Manage a stable of directors?

**It helps to...**
- Be pragmatic and organized.
- Have a good head for business and a good eye for creativity.
- Have a good understanding of the latest hardware and software in your trade.

**In high school you can...**
- Make and shoot videos for all local bands.
- Help coordinate the filming of live events.
- Oversee the production of your school's talent show, pageant or other events.

## VIDEO DIRECTOR

Although video directors can work with journalists (or as a journalists themselves), there's another, more unique and ultimately artistic way to use one's talent in creating motion pictures: directing music videos.

A music video director is charged with creating a visual concept to accompany an artist's musical work. Often used as a promotional tool, music videos are meant to market, stylize and enhance feelings about the artist in a positive way. Many music video directors go on to work in other high-concept media, such as advertising. Some even make feature films!

**Are you ready to...**

- Create a visual companion to an artist's music?
- Work with the musicians, other actors, extras, set designers and crew to realize that vision?
- Manage complex video shoots under tight deadlines?
- Spend long hours editing video?
- Work with both the artist's and the record label's marketing department to create an effective promotional piece?

**It helps to...**

- Have a good visual eye and a creative storytelling mind.
- Have a good understanding of the history of the genre.
- Be able to visualize a song's meaning or feeling.
- Know the basics of film production and editing.
- Be able to work with a diverse array of people—including some with strong opinions and big egos!

**In high school you can...**

- Take your video camera everywhere. Learn to make the most ordinary settings seem exciting on camera.
- Take photo and video editing classes.
- Make a music video—or take live concert footage—for a local band.

## RADIO

The world of radio is an intricate blend of music promotions, marketing and advertising created to stimulate listener attention, brand loyalty and artist appreciation. When you're listening to the radio in your car, you may not realize the complex structure and functions that are behind the music and advertisements you hear. In radio, there's opportunity in many business areas. We've already discussed the ones that involve being a radio journalist, and as with magazines and TV stations, radio companies also have avertising sales teams, etc. Some other radio jobs include:

- **DISC JOCKEY/HOST:** Choose and play recordings on the air. Today, many disc jockeys play music from preset playlists.
- **PROGRAMMER/PROGRAM DIRECTOR:** Choose the recordings that DJs will play and create playlists.
- **SOUNDBOARD OPERATOR:** Mix the sound, combining music, live voice (DJ or host), prerecorded advertisements, etc.
- **PRODUCER:** Oversee both content and technical aspects of each radio show and book guests for the host to interview.
- **AUDIO EDITOR:** Prepare pre-recorded spots (like ads, bumpers and station IDs) for air.

### Are you ready to...

- Use new music to engage fans and sell air-time?
- Always be promoting the station in bars, music venues, nightclubs and more?

■ Plan events, concerts and interviews at the station and other venues?

**It helps to...**

■ Enjoy selling and promoting your ideas.

■ Like interacting with people at live events.

■ Work well within a bureaucratic system with many co-workers.

**In high school you can...**

■ Work with local radio to sponsor your school's talent show or other events.

■ Create fan appreciation events around artist performances.

■ Volunteer to promote concerts at a local venue.

# Looking Ahead

Like the music industry, the media business is in a period of great transition. Established outlets like newspapers and broadcast TV networks no longer dominate mass communication. Online and mobile outlets, blogs, and even informal social media have opened many doors to new voices, while technology that combines text, images, audio and video have redefined the word "journalist." But the role of media—to deliver information to an intended audience—will never change. The better you understand your subject and the more clearly you explain your facts or opinions, the better your chance of finding and building that audience.

# EDUCATION

**M**usic education is a unique field, if for no other reason than that the definition of "music teacher" can vary widely. Some teachers have never been onstage in a professional setting; others are virtuoso performers. Some teachers have masters degrees and even PhDs in music and music education; others are self-taught players with many hours of stage experience behind them. Some work in public or private schools as a part of the larger education system, and others work for independent music schools and conservatories, or give lessons at local music stores. Some teachers—especially those who perform or record regularly—operate their business to combine teaching with "performance clinics" that demonstrate technique as well as a sponsor's piece of gear. A growing number of music teachers focus on things that were once ignored by the formal curriculum: pop music, music technology, recording, sound design and more.

In other words: There's room for just about everyone to do everything. You could teach a student to play an instrument, make an instrument, conduct, compose, arrange or use software. You could teach areas of music business, history, journalism, theory, composition—the list goes on.

The thread that binds the members of this field together is a passion for teaching and sharing knowledge and experience. The ultimate goal is to prepare young minds and nurture their interests for a potential career in music.

There is no substitution for real world experience, and a growing number of college programs are becoming increasingly interested in professional experience in addition to degrees. Unlike the music industry, where the majority of people do not have degrees in music, teaching music requires a much more specified degree. For example, you don't need a music degree to run a record label, but you do need a PhD. to teach ethnomusicology at a university.

It is widely held that education is a meaningful and rewarding field, and most teachers—myself included—recognize how powerful the transfer of knowledge can be. There's an opportunity for teachers to learn as well: As we teach, we're getting a point of view from a younger student, which often speaks to the zeitgeist of a generation. The music business is constantly evolving and changing; oftentimes key decisions are largely driven by youth culture. Music has always been defined by the innovation of a few key pioneers. As a teacher, you have the ability to influence this innovation and see new ideas from their inception through their execution.

There's an important vicarious element to student success that often takes hold when teaching. Chris Sampson from the University of Southern California's Thornton School of Music describes that feeling, saying, "Little did I know that I'd take far more pleasure in seeing my students succeed than having my own personal performance success."

Many people teaching business on the collegiate level feel that they are sustaining and furthering their field through education. Years ago, there existed no proper training for the music industry. Now, music educators are innovating to best prepare their students at all different levels, even incorporating an element of entrepreneurship to the curriculum.

Teaching music doesn't mean that you're restricted to the classroom; many music educators simultaneously maintain professional careers in and out of the classroom—whether it's conducting an orchestra, running the division of a record label or producing new albums. Middle school band teachers may spend the day teaching their students, but they may also play concerts within multiple ensembles at night. In addition to conventional classroom education, some educators give private lessons or tutorials on the side.

There exists incredible opportunity within the field of education—so much so that you'll often be able to create your own niche and pursue any number of interests. Whether you're an arts administrator also writing for a music blog, or an events manager also playing in a prestigious orchestra, the educational field is one of the best avenues to explore your many talents and passions.

# Private Practice

Private music teachers can run the complete gamut in experience and teaching methods. Many are formally educated and may work for a school district, conservatory or university in addition to teaching privately. Others are simply musicians with a passion for teaching.

Teaching privately can be a great way to start; high school kids with a decent grasp of their own instrument might want to teach younger beginners (or even their own friends). They may also be able to get a chance to teach at local camps and other opportunities.

Here are a few of the disciplines that fall under private teachers:

## INSTRUMENT OR VOICE TEACHER

Whether formally trained or self taught, an instrument or voice teacher should at least understand the basics of technique and accepted practice. New teachers can use method books for a guide to help shape the lessons. The advantage of being an individual instrument or voice teacher is that you can shape the lessons to meet the skill level and requirements of the student. A guitar teacher, for example, can create one curriculum for a student interested in blues, and another for someone who wants to master theory and scales.

Independent music teachers can work in a variety of settings, and not all of them are in the classroom. *Clinics*, for example, involve teaching a group, often in music stores or at events like trade shows and conventions. Some teachers work with professionals. Of these, *vocal coaches* are the most common.

Then there are the many online opportunities for teaching. For example, you can post lessons on YouTube, or use Skype or another video service to give one-on-one lessons.

**Are you ready to...**

- Work closely with a wide range of students that vary in ability?
- Create your own lesson plans that match the students' needs and ability?
- Market yourself to prospective students or to private music schools and music stores?
- Use technology to reach students?

**It helps to be...**

- Personable and patient.
- Able to adapt teaching methods for individual students.
- Up-to-date on musical styles and techniques.
- Well-organized and good at both marketing yourself and running your own business.

**In high school you can...**

- Start giving lessons to beginners.
- Study method books to use as a guide for building your own lessons.

■ Take private lessons and talk to your teacher about his or her teaching methods.

# School Music Teacher

There are many different opportunities that fall under the spectrum of teaching: You can work at the elementary, middle or high school levels, and you can teach a wide range of classes. Whether you're a band, chorus or orchestra director—or a teacher of general music, music history, or work with the marching band, musical theater, or music technology programs—the necessary skills and characteristics of the job remain similar.

**Are you ready to...**

■ Work closely with a wide range of students that vary in ability and motivation?

■ Grade papers, tests and homework, review practice sheets and conduct performance assessments?

■ Communicate with parents about the progress of their children and hold parent-teacher conferences?

**It helps to be...**

■ Dedicated to helping students succeed.

■ Extremely patient when working with students that may learn at a slower rate than their peers.

■ Creative in the way you convey information to keep your classes fun and engaging.

■ Knowledgeable about the latest teaching methods and academic standards.

**In high school you can...**

- Perform in your band, orchestra or chorus, and pay close attention to the learning process: Remember what exercises and methods helped you the most and which ones were least effective.
- Volunteer to student-teach at a local elementary school.
- Take lessons—or teach lessons—at your local music store.

# Higher Education

Higher education in music spans a variety of programs for BA, BM, and BFA degrees. There are two basic types of programs: conservatories and contemporary music programs. Conservatory program curriculum focuses on theory and composition in classical and jazz genres. Contemporary programs offer diverse areas of learning in songwriting, music business and production.

## PROFESSOR

Professors of music in higher education work with students fully committed to entering the music business in one future capacity or another. As such, their curriculum is usually specific, career-oriented and based in the field of their own experience. A college class is the last stop for future music professionals before they enter the career world. As a professor you are fully committed to serving the needs of your students, oftentimes broadening your own knowledge of the industry to best prepare those you are entrusted to educate.

**Are you ready to...**

- Develop curriculum and syllabi with faculty members in order to create interesting courses for your students?
- Conduct your own research while mentoring others' research?
- Teach classes, give guest lectures and advise students?

**It helps to...**

- Be knowledgeable in many different fields related to music—whether it's business, technology, history or otherwise.
- Have a strong grasp on public speaking, from writing lectures to delivering them in an engaging way.
- Be patient in explaining difficult ideas or concepts.

**INSIDE STORY**

**CHRIS SAMPSON**
Educator
**USC Thornton School of Music**

*"I believe very much in being a student-centered teacher, meaning that my students are the providers of information as much as I'm the provider for them."*

**Areas that you can teach...**

- Conservatory and performance studies
- Music business
- History and criticism
- Ethnomusicology
- Technology and production

**In high school you can...**

- Listen to music from all genres and time periods in order to get a strong understanding of music history.
- Perform in your band, orchestra or chorus and audition at the regional and state levels.

## ARTS ADMINISTRATORS

The role of arts administrators can vary widely depending on the organization that they work for, but many of the daily responsibilities are similar, such as working on fundraising campaigns, managing the organization's staff and managing the budget.

**Are you ready to...**

- Develop strategic and creative fundraising campaigns?
- Serve as the face of your organization when dealing with members, potential members, news sources, the Board of Directors and more?
- Determine the best events for your program that fall within your budget?

**It helps to...**

- Have a strong interest in the arts combined with a business mentality.
- Be able to work equally as well with people from creative and business fields.
- Have strong organizational skills and the ability to manage multiple projects simultaneously.

**In high school you can...**

- Organize or participate in fundraisers for your school's cultural programs (such as theater, band or dance).
- Take arts classes as well as business classes.
- Help organize events such as concerts, open mic nights, readings, etc.

## GRANT WRITERS

Non-profit cultural institutions rely heavily upon grants to receive funding. If you're an arts administrator seeking funding for a certain project, you may find yourself writing grants to seek out sources of money and apply for fundraising on behalf of your organization.

**Are you ready to...**

- Write and edit grant proposals and detailed applications?
- Use databases specific to grant-funding in order to find all sources available for funding your organization?
- Develop ideas for alternative sources of funding?

**It helps to...**

- Have strong professional writing skills.
- Be detail-oriented and able to point out small errors in punctuation, spelling and grammar.
- Know how to effectively and concisely communicate an organization's goals and ideas.

**In high school you can...**

- Practice grant writing by applying for as many scholarships and fellowships as you can.
- Familiarize yourself with the many online databases available to grant writers.
- Hold a leadership role in a club and apply for funding through your school for events.

## EVENTS/CONCERT SERIES MANAGER

Many universities with music departments host a number of performances, lectures and other related events throughout the school year. Concert series managers are behind the scenes of all of these, helping to organize the details necessary to successfully execute the events.

**Are you ready to...**

- Schedule concerts that are relevant for your students and faculty that fit within the department's budget?
- Work with facilities managers, booking agents, tour managers, concert promoters and other events-related staff members?
- Hold dialogue with faculty members and department staff in order to gauge the best events for the department?

**It helps to...**

- Have a background in music and performance as well as strong administrative skills.
- Understand the interests of your department's faculty and students.
- Be highly organized and able to manage multiple calendars of events.

**In high school you can...**

- Assist with the organization of your school's talent show or concert series.
- Help local bands schedule performances in your area.

■ Hold a leadership position in student government that allows you to help plan events for the entire class.

## Looking Ahead

Music education is steeped in tradition but in recent years has begun to recognize the value of more contemporary musical styles as well as the technology used to create them. As a result, an understanding of as many genres as possible—and an ability to evolve while navigating the sometimes tricky academic landscsape—will enhance your chances for a long career in music education.

# CONCERTS
# AND EVENTS

**A**n amazing symphony of events must happen before the lights go on and you see an artist on stage at a concert—massive amounts of planning, organizing and promotion are required for a single show, let alone a tour, to be successful. The live area probably has the biggest "behind the scenes" component of any sector in the music industry.

The live touring industry is generally formed by a subculture of people, many of whom have a tattoo that fittingly explains life on the road: "A pirate's life for me." They spend endless hours traveling; it can be exhilarating, it can be lonely, and it can be any number of emotions in between. Different towns, different nights, the set up, the breakdown…there's a central paradox in the events industry: Many describe a certain monotony to the job, despite being in different locations and performing different shows every night. You'll often do the same routine night after night, but you'll be doing them in new places, generally getting to witness—or even explore— different cultures and landscapes as you go.

What's great about the live music industry is that it's very cyclical and freelance. Things open up regularly; many people enjoy this lack of permanence and the sense of freedom it brings. It allows you to work with different tours, and alongside different people. In a given year, you could be on three different tours with different types of music, different markets and different cities.

If you love the music business but can't stand being in the office, this is the job for you: You live in hotels, sleep in a bus and eat takeout constantly. If you're just starting off in the business, a job in live events is a great experience because it's easy to break into as a low-level employee. You can occupy the position of an assistant, a runner or another entry-level position with relative ease.

Touring is a unique way to learn about all aspects of the industry; any job in the events area will teach you about every other job in the events industry. Throughout your experience you will learn the roles of various occupations, which makes for a great starting point in the industry. As you get older, you can follow the example of many others who've used the experience they gained on the road to pursue careers in management, media, production, record labels, education and other sectors of the music industry. There's plentiful opportunity for growth in live music once you understand its inner workings.

Often times there are no educational requirements and very few organized training grounds for this kind of work. You simply need to go out and do it, starting at the bottom and working your way up. If you like being self-employed and enjoy being independent—but also enjoy the camaraderie of the band and touring environment—then this is a great fit for you.

There's something incredibly satisfying about your work when the show hits the stage. As Doug Nightwine—a tour manager, production manager and front-of-house engineer says, "The downbeat of the show: That's the payoff of everything you've done all day and the weeks leading up to it." But life on the road can also be tough. As Jackson Browne sang in "Stay," "Let the roadies take the stage/Pack it up and tear it down/They're the first to come and the last to leave/Working for that minimum wage."

People in the concert business might work directly for one artist, for a company representing a group of artists, for one venue, for a company representing a group of venues or for a company that provides services for artists (and their reps), venues or both.

In terms of function, there's a lot of overlap among possible employers. A sound technician, for example, does pretty similar work whether he's employed by an artist, a venue or a sound company renting his services and equipment. Booking agents employed by venues work similarly to the agents who work for artists. They set up their tours, but do it from a different perspective. Accountants, crew, lighting technicians and even merchandise salespeople use essentially the same skills no matter whom they work for.

You can, however, divide the concert and events business into three distinct categories: Business/planning, technical crew and support and creative.

# The Business End

Many things must happen before a tour can even begin to get started. The people who oversee it all are essential to the success of any live event. Good management and logistics are important, both behind the scenes and at the venue.

Here are some of the essential jobs on the business end.

## AGENT

An agent is primarily responsible for the planning, routing, scheduling and collecting of monies on an artist's tour. They find opening acts for existing clients, issue contracts and ensure that promoters and venues pay artists for performances. At major agencies—such as the Creative Artists Agency (CAA) or the William Morris Endeavor (WME)—music agents work in tandem with affiliated agents (branding, theatrical, film, TV) to help secure and promote clients in ancillary businesses.

**Are you ready to...**

■ Work with venues, clubs, promoters, tour managers and talent buyers to handle all aspects of the live experience?

■ Create a strategic, financially successful touring plan?

■ Work with record companies, radio stations and retail outlets to efficiently promote and market the live performance in popular cities?

**You should be...**

■ A dedicated fan of live music.

■ Able to work well with artist managers, club managers, talent bookers and promoters.

■ Able to see the long-term vision for an artist's touring strategy, including a strong grasp of financial considerations.

**In high school you can...**

■ See as many bands as possible.

■ Meet as many club owners and bookers as possible.

■ Critique different clubs: How's the sound, the lighting, the location? Pay close attention to different elements that make a show experience meaningful.

## PROMOTER/BOOKING AGENT

The main job of a promoter is to publicize the concert or event. Promoters are ultimately responsible for building a show's live audience and booking venues that fit the artist. They work with bands, clubs and agents to schedule performances.

**Are you ready to...**

■ Publicize events through word of mouth, paid advertisements, blogs, concert listings and more?

■ Curate events on local and national levels?

■ Work long, often irregular, hours late into the night?

**It helps to be...**

■ A fan of live music with an intimate understanding of the details relevant to concerts and tours.

■ Good at conflict resolution, whether it's between the band, club, manager or another party.

■ Outgoing—able to meet and interact with people easily.

**In high school you can...**

■ Throw events at your high school or local clubs.

■ Curate an all-ages show with local bands and DJs.

■ Establish relationships with all of the venues in your town.

### INSIDE STORY

**DOUG NIGHTWINE**
**Tour Manager**

*"You'll be the first guy into the venue every day, introducing yourself to the dozen or so people that are the heads of the local staffing you hired. No matter how you design the show, there are always changes you'll have to make--you are always infinitely adjusting every element. It's an ever-changing world, and it's never the same twice."*

## TOUR MANAGER

The tour manager is the senior person responsible for every aspect of the tour's success. From budgets and hotels to sound and lighting, this person is the eyes and ears of the artist's manager while the artist is on tour.

"The most interesting parts of the job are the people you meet on the road," says veteran tour manager Chris Alderman. "You go to different regions of the U.S. as well as Canada, Australia, Japan and other locations. Just seeing the different cultures within the US and overseas, and within the group dynamics of a crew, is incredible: It's being a part of something bigger than just playing a show for music."

## MERCHANDISE SALES

The sale of merchandise—things like T-shirts and other apparel, calendars, posters, programs, stickers and other souveniers—is a major source of income for performing artists. (In fact, even an up-and-coming act can do well and build its fan base through merchandise.) As a result, there are many opportunities within this field. You can be the artist who creates the merchandise (see "Graphic Design" in Chapter 9: Media) or the individual selling it at a venue. There are also positions dedicated to finding great non-traditional merchandise products to fit specific artists and fan bases.

Someone must manage getting the merchandise to the venue, setting it up for display and sale, tracking the inventory and sales, collecting money and then packing the leftovers up for next time.

Selling the merchandise itself—working the "merch booth"—is a great entry level

**INSIDE STORY**

**CHRIS ALDERMAN**
**Tour manager**

*"Your day looks like this: Post a schedule for everybody first thing in the morning. Organize a meet and greet with guests for the artist. Most importantly, do the accounting of the day by collecting the guarantee or finding out what we make at the door, then making sure everyone gets on the bus for the next show. The most important thing is being able to keep all lines of communication open to band, crew, with management, booking agent. And it's not all the same information that needs to be conveyed to each person. Communication and organization are key, so you're providing the right info to the right people. The toughest part of the job is hiring good people around you, because that's what makes a crew a crew."*

position for those interested in touring and music business in general.

**Are you ready to...**

- Be involved with or oversee the production, shipping and distribution of merchandise?
- Deal with venues, retail outlets and consumers?

**It helps to be...**

- Realistic about product costs and able to predict which items will sell successfully.
- Financially mindful and able to manage profit margins.
- Up to date on consumer trends and products in retail.

**In high school you can...**

- Design and sell merchandise for your school, local bands, church or clubs.
- Create a website that sells merchandise for local acts.
- Learn about design and illustration software.
- Work at a retail outlet.
- Work (or volunteer) in the merch booth at local shows.

## ARTIST ASSISTANT

The assistant serves as the right hand of an artist. Responsibilities can range from grunt work tasks to acting as a conduit between the artist and other important parties. This is very much a precursor to artist management and can serve as a great learning curve.

**Are you ready to...**

- Work around the clock, always on call?
- Travel extensively?
- Learn all aspects of the music industry through the artist's experience?
- Handle confidential situations and conversations with discretion?

**It helps to be...**

- A solution-oriented problem solver.
- Level-headed; you should able to deal well with stressful situations.
- A-type personality; you should be able to take charge of situations easily.

**In high school you can...**

- Intern for a local executive or business owner in an assistant capacity.
- Work for your local radio station on DJ appearances and promotions.
- Serve as manager for one of your school clubs and manage events.
- Serve as team manager for one of your school's sports teams.

# Stage Crew and Technical Staff

The stage crew is responsible for getting a venue ready for a performance. At a small club, one person may be responsible for many things—from sound to lights to setting up the venue's backline of amps and drums. On a large tour, a team of people work together. Here are a few of the key jobs.

## SOUND ENGINEER

Sound engineers are responsible for the overall sonic experience of a live show. They handle all aspects of sound, starting with the soundcheck and continuing throughout the performance. There's a lot to do: You must get all the onstage sounds through the house system, set the level of all the instruments and microphones and mix the show as it happens. On larger tours, a separate engineer may be responsible for the sound going to the audience (known as front-of-house, or FOH) and another may focus on setting up the performer's monitors so that they can hear themselves onstage. Many bands consider the sound engineer to be the most important member of the band during show time.

Most live sound engineers get their start locally, either working with area acts or using the in-house sound system at area clubs. At first, you might serve as a sound engineer and a member of the crew, responsible for setting everything up as well as managing the sound. In addition to working at a local club or for an artist, other possible employers include sound/lighting companies; these companies hire engineers to run their equipment and work their festivals. One sound company might handle multiple acts, theaters, concert halls and other performance spaces with permanently installed equipment.

**Are you ready to...**

■ Be responsible for the sound quality of concerts?

- Make quick decisions and adjustments on the fly during concerts?
- Spend late nights at clubs listening to bands or spend months (even years in some cases) on the road mixing the same band?

**You should...**

- Understand microphone placement and other basic sound engineering techniques.
- Be knowledgeable about live mixing boards, PA systems, the latest technology and techniques.
- Have confidence and trust in your ears when making quick decisions during live shows.
- Be able to use the tools at hand to enhance the concert experience.
- Be good at solving unexpected problems very quickly.

**In high school you should...**

- Get to know sound engineers at local clubs.
- Do live sound for local musicians.
- Study the basics of sound engineering.
- Learn the sonic pros and cons of different venue spaces. Develop an understanding of how a venue's layout and architecture affects the sound.
- Work live sound at school events.

## INSTRUMENT TECHNICIAN

When you go to a concert and see people on stage setting up instruments before the band plays, chances are you're looking at instrument technicians ("techs" for short). Behind the scenes, they are tuning instruments, calibrating equipment and getting gear prepared for the concert. Many techs are players themselves, specializing in one instrument or another. They understand not only how to take care of the instrument(s) but also how to fine-tune them to their client's liking.

**Are you ready to...**

- Become intimately familiar with a specific instrument and the accessories or supporting gear needed for an artist or show?
- Repair broken or malfunctioning gear in the field?
- Efficiently execute important daily maintenance tasks such as restringing guitars, tuning drums, setting up keyboards, checking and maintaining amps, etc.?
- Organize and manage a performer's equipment, assuring that everything is ready to go before each show?

**It helps to be...**

- Extremely knowledgeable about music equipment, but able to communicate that knowledge to band members in understandable terms.
- Good at trouble-shooting when gear is not working properly.
- A player yourself, able to analyze how well instruments and equipment are working based on the client's needs (and not your own).

**In high school you can...**

- Work in a music store's sales or repair department.
- Help bands prepare their equipment before live shows.
- Experiment with building and customizing musical instruments and equipment.

## LIGHTING TECHNICIAN

When you go to a concert, much of the live experience is drawn from lighting. For live events, lighting can make or break a show. The lighting technician's job is to make sure that the lights are used to enhance the show, not simply to make it visible.

In clubs, lighting is usually handled in-house (sometimes by a sound engineer). On major tours, lighting is carefully designed and often choreographed in exact detail. The lighting team is part of the tour itself.

**Are you ready to...**

- Learn how to operate complex lighting equipment?
- Create the visual setting for live music events?
- Spend a significant amount of time on the road?
- Hit precise lighting cues every night?

**It helps to...**

- Have a passion for visual arts, graphic design and film.
- Be able to connect music with relevant visual cues.
- Be knowledgeable in the use of control equipment.

**In high school you can...**

- Study how lighting is used in videos and concert footage.
- Get involved with lighting school productions.
- Get a job with a local events production company.
- Attend concerts and try to talk to the lighting crew.

## OTHER CREW AND SUPPORT JOBS

In addition to the jobs that relate directly to the way shows are presented, many tours carry additional staff, including:

- **ROADIE**: On big tours, roadies do the heavy lifting—literally. They help set up the stages, move the gear on and off the trucks, and keep everything in order. Unlike the instrument technicians, who are also part of the road crew, roadies don't need to be able to play the instruments. But they do need to be strong, reliable and disciplined.

- **VIDEO CREW**: Many large shows now feature live video, shown on big screens, which allows the audience in the so-called "cheap seats" to see the show. Tours will often carry several camera operators and a director to make it all happen.

- **SECURITY**: Protect the artists and/or their equipment.

- **CATERING**: Usually hired by the venue, provide food and drink to the crew.

- **DRIVERS**: Drive tour buses and equipment vans. Sometimes, this is handled by a roadie.

# Creative

Putting on a great show requires an intense amount of creative planning, offering opportunities in visual design and performance. Here are a few creative jobs in the live concert business.

## TOURING MUSICIAN ("THE HIRED GUN")

Touring musicians (also known as "sidemen") are hired for their look, their personality, their skill and how well they fit with an artist's act. The most talented musicians aren't always the ones who get the gig: Touring musicians have to blend in with the band, play the music the band plays in the style that they play and dress like they dress. Touring musicians should seem indistinguishable from the rest of the band during live shows.

**Are you ready to...**

- Tour consistently and play tons of live shows?
- Be a background member of the band rather than the superstar?
- Learn to adjust your playing style or aesthetic according to the needs of the bands you're playing with?

**It helps to...**

- Be extremely proficient with the instrument(s) and styles that you play.
- Be able to quickly and thoroughly learn new material in any style required.
- Have the ability to work well with other musicians,

both personally and musically.
- Be reliable and consistent.

**In high school you can...**
- Form your own band and play local venues.
- Rehearse with or sit in on sessions with local bands.
- Seek out opportunities with musicians in your area to play live shows.
- Study every style possible on your instrument and develop strong reading skills.

## SHOW DESIGNER

While it's true that some artists seem to simply get onstage and play, most major tours—especially those headlined by artists with a theatrical flair—present carefully designed shows that are the product of a long creative process. From stage design to visual effects, from stage props to choreography, from lighting decisions to the overall aesthetic—the show designer puts together the various elements of a live production to make it exciting and memorable.

**Are you ready to...**
- Bring your artistic vision to life on stage in front of large crowds?
- Work closely with musicians to enhance their performance with compelling visuals?
- Work closely with a team of choreographers, lighting technicians and sound engineers?

**It helps to...**

- Understand how visual elements can enhance music.
- Develop a vision for stages of various sizes and music of various styles.
- Be able to manage many creative personalities in a collaborative environment.

**In high school you can...**

- Go to every big arena, amphitheater or stadium show possible.
- Watch, rent or view every concert DVD available: Take note of the details that make a show memorable.
- Work for an events production company to get a feel for the industry.
- Stage manage a musical production at your school.

## SET BUILDING AND STAGE DESIGN

As a stage designer, you are responsible for creating the interface that presents the artist to the audience. There's a wide range of opportunity in this field: For example, you can design stages for clubs in addition to major performance structures that go on tour with acts. Set design—adding elements to an existing stage—can be a combination of carpentry, manual labor, and aesthetic creativity.

On many larger tours, the stage is carried to the venue and set up every night by a dedicated crew. In these cases, the designer is more of an architect than a builder. His or her job is to create a design with materials that will not only look good, but that will be safe and transportable. The set must be easy to set up and break down in a reasonable amount of time by readily available crew.

**Are you ready to...**

- Sketch out a workable plan for a stage?
- Work with your hands?
- Master different building materials?
- Learn to read design plans?

**It helps to...**

- Be knowledgeable about design and carpentry.
- Be a strong mathematician, able to understand angles and measurements.
- Have a lot of experience with live performances.

**In high school you should...**

- Take any shop or stage design classes that your school offers.
- Volunteer to build the set for school productions.
- Work in construction as a summer job.

# Looking Ahead

Concerts and touring have become important revenue streams for artists in recent years, and this has affected the whole of the music businesses. Major tours are bigger than ever, but small and midsized venues also offer notable opportunities. On the local scene, live music tends to ebb and flow over time. Club DJs have become increasingly popular, especially in certain cities, but you may also find emerging trends like acoustic music, live jazz and even classical music presented in clubs.

One of the best ways to get your feet wet is to try producing shows yourself. Get together with friends and promote a concert or DJ night at a party. Many of today's industry leaders started just that way.

# 11

# ENTREPRENEURIAL

**T**he entrepreneurial spirit is alive and thriving in the music industry right now. With the increasing accessibility of technology, the playing field has been leveled in many ways: When a good idea meets great execution—that's the birthplace of success. Artists no longer have managers; they have partners. And record deals often resemble brand agreements more than recording contracts.

Now is the perfect time for people with self-confidence, a strong vision, knowledge, motivation and organization to start their own companies. When your grandparents were growing up, it took a lifetime to build a company; now, it can take less than five years to build a hugely successful organization. The time it takes to be successful has diminished dramatically.

The paths of entrepreneurs are as diverse as the ideas that they bring to fruition: There's no single answer to the question, "How can I become a successful entrepreneur?" There are the famous anecdotes about figures like Bill Gates and Steve Jobs—two of America's most successful entrepreneurs, and not a college degree between them.

On the other hand, you have someone like Jeff Bezos, the founder of Amazon.com. He did get a formal education: He attended Princeton University, where he graduated summa cum laude and Phi Beta Kappa. Successful entrepreneurs can stem from any variety of backgrounds, so long as they are entirely dedicated to the pursuit of their vision. Whether you're academically inclined or not, whether you're tech-savvy or not, whether you're a first-generation immigrant or the grandchild of an American president, the entrepreneurial field is open to you if you possess the know-how and dedication to turn a great idea into a profitable business model.

## What's an Entrepreneur?

In simple terms, an *entrepreneur* is one who creates and runs his or her own business, sometimes working alone, sometimes building it up with associates, partners or employees. Entrepreneurs are innovators, and the most successful among them are the people who identify and exploit new opportunities that more established businesses ignore.

Generally, people associate the term "entrepreneurial" with the founders of Fortune 500 companies: the men and women who are responsible for starting huge, multi-national organizations. You'll see in this chapter, however, there are many types of people who embrace and embody the entrepreneurial spirit—not just the ones who appear on the cover of Forbes. From managers and lawyers to philanthropists and bloggers, the music industry is full of talented self-starters. You'll notice that many of the businesses listed here include jobs that we explored elsewhere in this book. Some entrepreneurs take an established skill, as well as experience gained working as an employee, and turn it into a successful business. Others invent new skills and business, responding to a need in the marketplace. Finally there are the select few who create the need themselves by coming up with a product or service in such demand that everyone has to have one. Don't believe me? Well, no one thought they "needed" a social networking site like Facebook until they learned of its existence. Now, hundreds of millions of people use the site every day. Undoubtedly, an entrepreneur was behind its creation.

Regardless of where your interests lie within the music business, if you're passionate about pursuing your ideas in a leadership role, this may be the area for you.

## ARTIST MANAGER

An artist manager's job is to oversee all aspects of a creative and business career in music. The manager is charged with the responsibility of furthering that career—from independent, DIY artists to multi-platinum superstars—in many capacities. Whether you're deciding the best label for an artist or helping to come up with a new image, managers help direct the business and creative aspects of an artist's career.

**Are you ready to...**

■ Be a jack-of-all-trades, necessary to the artist's success?

■ Allow your creative influence to shape the artist's career while always placing their vision first?

■ Serve as mediator between artist and other major parties like label reps, producers, booking agents, etc.?

## INSIDE STORY

**MICHAEL SOLOMAN**
Founder
**Brick Wall Management**

*"Talking to clients about strategy and direction is a key thing. I think there are so many changes going on in any given moment that if you don't spend active time figuring out what's coming, it's going to hit you in the head. There is nothing better than winning when you're a manager because your client is your partner; you've been through a lot together, which is usually not easy. When you're winning—not to make it competitive with everyone else—you're one in a million who's succeeding and that's a very powerful feeling. You need to be good at dealing with people who aren't always good at dealing with people."*

## INDEPENDENT LABEL OWNERS

As the owner of an independent label, you need to have an understanding of every element of the business, from creative to financial and anything in between. You have tremendous accountability, and with that comes the ability to make final decisions on big issues (see Chapter 4: Record Labels for an overview of this rapidly changing business).

**Are you ready to...**

■ Do every job—from CEO to receptionist?

■ Develop a vision for your company that includes feasible long-term plans as well as ways to handle the difficulties of starting up?

- Find artists and find ways to sell their music?
- Construct a team around your label, knowing when to delegate tasks?

**You should...**

- Have strong decision-making and multi-tasking abilities; the big decisions and heavy responsibilities will fall on you.
- Be able to manage people from diverse backgrounds.
- Have a grasp of both the business and creative sides of the music business.

**In high school you can...**

- Start your own label by creating a roster with local acts—help them book gigs, release music and build a fan base.
- Build a team of people to market and promote a local act.
- Familiarize yourself with the paths of successful independent labels.
- Take all business classes available to you.

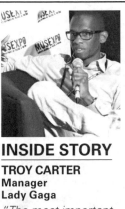

**INSIDE STORY**

**TROY CARTER**
**Manager**
**Lady Gaga**

*"The most important qualities are honesty and perseverance; really being able to stick at something when it feels like it isn't working. I think it's really about caring about what you do and caring about the people you work with. We all have to start somewhere—the ones who become great at business are the ones who really fought for and cared about the clients they worked with. The biggest challenges have been for people to see things that aren't currently there—to have people believe and invest in my vision."*

## SPECIALTY RETAIL SHOP OWNERS

Niche-oriented specialty shops are known for having hard-to-find items and eclectic products. These stores usually have a tight-knit, enthusiastic fan base and—when successful—can develop cult-followings. They can operate in physical locations or on the Internet.

### INSIDE STORY
**JOSH DEUTSCH**
**Founder**
**Downtown Records**

*"When you own your own label, you have to own every deal. I learned more in the first 15 months operating my own business than I did in my previous 15 years [working at previously established labels]."*

**Are you ready to...**

■ Become an expert in whatever you're selling?

■ Find your audience in the lifestyle arena?

■ Accept the limitations of your business and compete with much larger companies?

**You should be...**

■ Knowledgeable and specifically passionate about your product.

■ Able to curate across a wide-spectrum of genres, sub-genres and entities in order to cast as wide a net as possible.

■ Business-minded but able to cater to artistic customers.

**In high school you can...**

■ Get to know local independent record stores and specialty retail stores—if there are none where you live, find them online.

■ Participate in online communities, conferences and conventions in the area you're most interested in—such as the National Association for Retail Marketing.

■ Collect whatever retail you're interested in selling.

Whether it's vinyl, cassettes or picture discs—collect and trade. Be an active participant in your genre.

## STUDIO OWNERS

A studio owner is responsible for the booking, the maintenance and the upkeep of a recording studio. They choose a space, pay the rent and hire staff. A studio owner needs to know the latest technologies and techniques, as well as how to market their space to make it appealing to working producers and bands.

**In high school you can...**

- Set up a home studio and record local acts.
- Work in a managerial capacity at a local studio; handle bookings.
- Spend as much time as possible in the studio to get to know the ins and outs of daily operations.
- Take classes at a technical school for music production.

## THE ARTIST AS ENTREPRENEUR

While changes in the music industry have had a negative impact on the sale of recorded music, these same changes have created more oppor-

**INSIDE STORY**

**JOHN KIEHL**
**Co-founder Soundtrack Recording Studios**

*"The first thing I do in the morning is return all my phone calls and make all my phone calls. I can start doing that while I'm still in bed and I do. If you've agreed to do business with somebody you have to take the effort to contact that person. The typical day for me is talking to about 20 people—I might only get to 10 of those people in one day, but it's my job to realize that I never spoke to so-and-so to make sure this doesn't linger. I touch base with everybody I'm doing business with. At the end of the day, my success as a recording engineer comes from the same place that a chef's success comes from when he's cooking. It's all about taste and this artistic sensibility—the fact that he knows the boiling temperature of butter doesn't make him a good chef."*

tunities for artists than ever before. Artists can now achieve success on their own terms without the help of a label, but with this increased opportunity, artists must have a solid understanding of all areas in the business to truly make the most of their independent career. In order to be successful, an artist can no longer simply focus on his/her music; the entrepreneurial spirit must be present in order to achieve success in today's market place. This means an artist needs a good understanding of budgets, touring, social media, marketing, maybe even production and other industry sectors to find and communicate with new fans.

**Are you ready to...**

- Dedicate equal time and energy to creativity and business?
- Develop a solid, authentic brand and adhere to it in career choices?
- Take ultimate responsibility for your own success; be a self-starter and a creator of opportunity?

**You should be...**

- Aware of your career timeline; know when to build a team of like-minded industry professionals around your art to take your success to the next level.
- Able to create and adhere to a plan for business and creative growth.
- Willing to accept constructive criticism, constantly striving to be a better artist and businessperson.

**In high school you can...**

- Take business classes.
- Work to master your instrument or craft.
- Collaborate with other artists.

**Working Artists Perspectives**

Being a professional artist is difficult in and of itself, but it's especially hard if you overlook the "professional" part of the term. We asked several working artists how they go about their respective businesses.

"I have a piano in my house, so I spend an hour or so a day searching amongst the keys for chords, tones and melodies that are swimming in my head," Ryan Leslie says. "I engage myself in conversation with people that are going to inspire me. Through the years I've had some of the most incredible relationships—incredible because whether they worked out or went horribly wrong, they were absolutely inspiring. The rest of the bulk of my day is spent just looking at the feedback or impact that anything I've created has generated. I'm online and I'm looking at my various social media presences. That's also very encouraging because those metrics are very real and very tangible—in many ways fuel the creation of new art.

"The biggest surprise has been meeting my heroes and realizing that they're extremely human. You get to the industry, you finally get a chance to meet one of your entrepreneurial heroes or musical heroes, and realize that they've got the same amount of hours in the day as you have; they get tired and they get cranky and upset and frustrated and they get bogged down by the bureaucratic or political bottlenecks which restrict their creativity. That revelation is really enlightening."

"Be really nice to people and get along with people and treat everyone with respect no matter where they are in the pecking order," adds DJ Rekha. "You just have to have some hustle. You can't be afraid to do any aspect of the job at any point. I see a lot of people not willing to pay their dues and their time—there's a certain expectation or entitlement. It takes years and years to build relationships and contacts; it takes staying power."

## MUSIC SUPERVISOR

A music supervisor helps choose music for film, television and commercials. They work as a liaison between film/TV production companies, composers, artists and sound libraries.

In some cases, the music supervisor will also oversee the legal clearances necessary to insure that music can be used in certain productions.

**Are you ready to...**

■ Familiarize yourself with all styles and genres of music?

■ Watch a lot of film, television and

### INSIDE STORY

**MAUREEN CROWE**
Music Supervisor
GTM

*"Get involved in lots of musical productions. Learn how a show is put together and learn about the legalities of music. You shouldn't be downloading music for free. You could also shadow, wherever you are—shadow people for a day and learn what the relationships are between the music director and a client and producer. You could go in and follow people's careers and learn about what they're doing. There are books out there that you should read, and the Guild of Music Supervisors might be a good place to start. Experiment with different things. Make a movie with someone, take care of the music, play with it, have fun with it, learn that way. If you want to be a music supervisor, start doing it."*

commercials and decide the best music that fits each?

■ Work closely with music publishers to negotiate synchronization deals?

**You should be able to...**

■ According to music supervisor Maureen Crowe: "Work with a wide variety of personalities [and] be able to look at the whole picture as well as the very minute details."

■ Separate your personal taste from the needs of the project.

■ Maintain a highly organized system in order to keep track of the correspondence related to various licensing requests.

## STARTUP / BUSINESS OWNER

There's no shortage of great ideas out there—but businesses are made in the execution, not just in the concept.

You have to be able to translate an idea into action in any business—it doesn't matter if you're selling music or selling carpet. You need to be able to determine if an idea is financially feasible and profitable.

**INSIDE STORY**

**ARIEL HYATT**
Founder
**Ariel Publicity and CyberPR**

*"It's all about sales. It's all about really listening to what it is that potential clients want and what could potentially be sold in the future. You should be constantly writing, reading and researching. If you take your eyes off technology for even two weeks, you could get away from what's happening."*

**In high school you should...**

■ Read as many books and magazines as possible that cover innovators and business leaders.

- Run your own business, even if the project is on a small scale.
- Find something about your school, town or organization that you don't like or think can be improved upon, and come up with a business solution to fix it. Then act on it!

**INSIDE STORY**

**STEVE STOUTE**
Founder
**Translation Consulta-
tion and Brand Imaging**

*"Every day, you
should try to find
ideas. Try to find more
companies that are on
the verge of missing
the millennium
consumer due to not
necessarily paying
attention to that
consumer and
encouraging them to
do better. Be aware of
what's going on. You
need to understand
many different
business models. Part
of trying to find a
solution for a com-
pany is being able to
understand the
company's business
model. I never let my
personal taste affect
the target audience
we're going after
because it's their
taste I'm interested
in."*

## PHILANTHROPY

When working in philanthropy, you'll have the ability to work with others in a way that's entirely unique to the music business. You need an absolute passion for whatever it is that you're doing, and the job requires a huge amount of social entrepreneurship in order to raise money to help others. Successful philanthropists must have a clarity of vision that they're able to express to others.

**In high school you can...**

- Volunteer with a local philanthropy organization or join a service-oriented club at your school.
- Hold a fundraiser for a cause that you're dedicated to: Raise money by organizing a concert or other event.
- Take part in a local chapter of a national fundraising campaign (such as Red Cross, Doctors Without Borders or something similar).

## COMPOSER FOR MOTION PICTURES AND OTHER MEDIA

The composer is a sonic architect and performer for all forms of visual media, including film, television, commercials and advertisements. This is a highly lucrative and explosive area of growth in the music industry.

**Are you ready to...**

- Spend long hours composing and recording music?
- Write songs tailored very specifically toward certain themes or products?
- Accept rejection for music that you've written on a regular basis if the client doesn't feel it suits the need of the project?

**It helps to...**

- Pay attention to all of the music that you hear accompanying visual media.
- Be a musical chameleon: You should have a good idea of the sonic properties of a number of different genres.
- Purchase and listen to a number of soundtracks and television scores to acquaint yourself with the type of music you'll need to write.

### INSIDE STORY
**JENNIFER HOWELL**
Founder
The Art of Elysium

*"The majority of my job is managing and executing programs effectively, while at the same time giving the artists what they need and also helping out with creative content and creative fundraisers. We're constantly doing events and concerts. I have to find what music is new and what people are going to respond to in order to be aware of what's going on in Los Angeles and New York that's exciting enough to share with the kids. You must believe so strongly in the work and what you do. You have to truly believe that music has the ability to heal."*

**In high school you can...**

- Turn the volume down on your favorite films and television shows and compose your own music to accompany them.
- Write the music for a student short, film or production; write the music for any visual project that you can get your hands on.
- Study award-winning compositions and scores to develop an understanding of how music best connects to visual art.
- Take music theory classes.

## INDEPENDENT MUSIC ATTORNEY

Attorneys are legal representatives whose mission is to protect the rights of their clients—which can range from record labels to artists, to industry organizations, to managers and even to other lawyers! Specializing in negotiations, most attorneys have strong relationships with managers. In the music business, lawyers are relied upon for strong and persuasive relationships. Some even help artists in a managerial capacity.

**Are you ready to...**

- Spend an additional three years in school after finishing your undergraduate degree?
- Negotiate complex deals with difficult parties?
- Be the voice of reason and/or reality amongst an artist's team of advisors?

**It helps to be...**

- Detail-oriented and willing to do research.
- Passionate about law, a problem-solver.
- Committed to an artist's success, willing to go above and beyond normal expectations.

**In high school you can...**

- Be on your school's debate team.
- Intern at a local law office.
- Read industry trade magazines like *Billboard* to familiarize yourself with deals.

## Looking Ahead

Now is the time to launch your own music business venture. It used to take a generation to build a successful company, but now, in the digital age, we see companies skyrocketing to the Fortune 500 in just a few years. We are living in a time where good ideas and great execution get you ahead. This is the era of the entrepreneur.

---

**INSIDE STORY**

**DOUG DAVIS**
Attorney
The Davis Firm

*"It helps to build relationships. So many of the clients pay based on who has the better relationships at the company, whether it's in management, publishing or record labels. Being able to get the decision maker on the phone separates the lawyers who can close the deal from those who can't. Access is the biggest commodity that's traded in the music business. My threshold is, 'Is it sellable?' I remove my own personal taste from my practice. If there's a talented person and a deal to be made, I'll find that money like a bomb-sniffing dog whether or not I think their music is any good."*

# 12

# INSTRUMENTS AND EQUIPMENT

**N**o matter what kind of music you like, or what instrument you play, stop to consider one thing: There would not be *any* music industry if there were no instruments. A vast worldwide industry is responsible for designing, building and selling everything from electric guitars and basses to digital keyboards to traditional acoustic instruments like pianos, brass, woodwind, strings and percussion. Add in sound equipment like microphones, speakers and amplifiers, as well as software and accessories, and you have the musical instrument industry, also known as MI.

If you're an equipment junkie and you love music, this is an area where you can marry those two interests, bringing together brands with bands. This is an area where all kinds of backgrounds can serve the greater good: Great musicians go on to work as reps and salesman to market and promote new products. Genius designers and code writers all find a home under one roof, tied together by a common passion for music.

While the music industry is often accused of being fickle and in transition, the product manufacturing companies tend to provide a stable working environment for many employees.

The MI field offers an interesting mix of working environments, too. Large companies like Fender, Gibson, Yamaha, Roland and others may dominate the market, but small businesses can and do succeed. Two examples—Peavey and Paul Reed Smith (both founded by their namesakes)—went from independent small firms to worldwide players in a very short amount of time.

It's also a field with many different roles. You'll find single artisans capable of building a violin or guitar worth thousands of dollars on their own as well as factory workers helping to create parts for speakers and amplifiers on an assembly line. There are marketing people who work with rock stars—and others who work with local school districts.

Like record labels, musical instrument companies need writers and graphic designers. Many produce video and audio demos, as well as live demonstrations. Their legal teams protect patents and trademarks; their buyers scour the globe for materials; their research and development (R&D) teams invent new products, refine old products and design better ways to build.

# Business, Legal and Marketing

Like any other business, musical instrument manufacturing can involve a range of departments. Companies that make instruments have shops (small companies) or factories (large companies), which need to be equipped and managed. In some cases, the tools used to make the instruments must be custom designed.

## ACCOUNTING AND LEGAL

On the business end, the accounting and legal departments work in much the same way as their counterparts in the record or other music industries. One difference is that instead of protecting intellectual property like songs, they must protect patents and trademarks. They also must make sure that the company complies with regulations about importing and selling goods and raw materials.

## BUYER

Companies that use a lot of materials—for example, the wood used to make guitars—have departments responsible for finding and shipping the material to the factory. In some cases, this can involve international travel, since many of the woods used in instruments are found overseas.

**Are you ready to...**

- ■ Understand the specifications needed to build each component?
- ■ Find the required materials, sometimes traveling overseas to do so?

■ Negotiate a good price for the materials, often with foreign governments?

■ Arrange shipping to the factory?

■ Monitor the use so that there's enough material to work with but not so much that it uses storage space?

**In high school you can...**

■ Study geography and natural resources.

■ Learn about the materials used to make various instruments.

■ Explore renewable resources that may be used to make instruments in the future.

## BRANDING AND MARKETING

These specialists are trusted advisors and confidants to the clients they represent, and they are expected to provide sound corporate guidance while providing up-to-the-moment cultural translations of trends, movements and phenomena affecting the health of the brand. Many of the people working in instrument marketing are musicians themselves. Some companies have separate departments that work with media, buyers (that is, retailers) and artists, but they're all devoted to the same goal: getting the product out there.

**Are you ready to...**

■ Have a foot in both the music world and the advertising world?

■ Represent the taste of the consumer, which may not necessarily align with your own?

- ■ Think of innovative ways to present a product to consumers?

**In high school you can...**

- ■ Pay attention to how your favorite brands use advertisements: Analyze their celebrity endorsements, the tone of their ads and their overall marketing strategies.
- ■ Put together an event with local bands and local businesses that is mutually beneficial.

## ARTIST RELATIONS

These industry professionals represent equipment companies to the music community at large and to individual artists. Among other things, they assure that artists are using updated versions of their company's products, coordinate product placements, arrange photo shoots and assure that artists' needs for live performance are met by their company's products. Artist relations representatives interact with both management and artists directly. They are responsible for creating effective artist endorsements—the number one way equipment companies market themselves to the public.

**INSIDE STORY**
**STEVE ARMSTRONG**
**Director of Marketing**
**Pearl Drums**

*"Devotion to the product makes a big difference. The level of passion people have for music makes these jobs extraordinary. We know in marketing that our job is a support staff to make sure that sales can do their jobs... if they aren't making the cash register 'caaa-ching', we're out of a job. You need a thick skin, a positive attitude and a willingness to work really hard. Everyone in this industry is working twice as hard as they did a few years ago."*

**Are you ready to...**

- ■ Travel around the country to see a lot of live music?

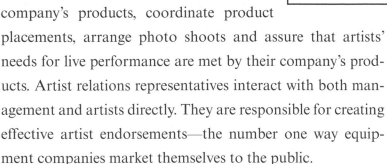

- Work closely with artists (and their teams) to facilitate product placements?
- Be a constant advocate, and a user yourself, of your company's products?

### It helps to...

- Be an effective communicator with an outgoing personality.
- Have broad-base knowledge of music instruments and the various companies that manufacture them.
- Be an adept musician yourself so that you can effectively communicate about, and advocate for, your product.

### In high school you can...

- Read instrument-specific magazines to understand which types of artists endorse which types of brands.
- Work at a local musical instrument store.
- Develop relationships with musicians to better understand their needs and preferences; you should understand why they choose one brand of instrument over another.

## SALES

The musical instrument industry is very competitive, so sales can be especially challenging. You need to understand all of the key marketing points for every instrument in the company's line and be able to present it to customers while knowing the cusomer's needs. At larger companies, the customers are usually retailers or institutions (like schools). Smaller companies often sell directly to consumers. The Internet is changing the job of sales as well, so you need to study trends and identify markets.

# Design and Execution

The business people wouldn't have much to do if it weren't for the people who invent, design and create the equipment, whether it's hardware, instruments, software, replacement parts, amplifiers, recording equipment, microphones, cases or the myriad of other accessories that musicians need.

## SOFTWARE DESIGNER

The innovator responsible for building and coding new ideas. This is fundamentally the technological side to a music idea. Behind every great music application on your phone and computer, there was a software designer and programmer who made it possible.

**Are you ready to...**

- Bring great ideas to digital life?
- Spend hours in front of a computer?
- Work long hours in a solitary environment?

**It helps to be...**

- Extremely computer savvy.
- A user of many technological apps.
- Interested in writing software code.
- Able to work well independently.

**In high school you can...**

- Take computer software classes at your high school, a technical institute or a vocational school.
- Begin designing your own applications and/or games.
- Play video games and get involved in the tech/coding culture.

## EQUIPMENT DESIGN AND CREATION

Musicians have always been hungry for new equipment—be it instruments or high technology—and it takes a combination of creativity and practicality to design products that will both appeal to artists and consumers—and perform in professional situations.

While certain products have maintained a timeless aesthetic—like a Fender Stratocaster—other areas of the industry require constant updating and design improvement (you may have noticed that there are *many* variations to that venerable Stratocaster, including versions that can work with synthesizers). Digital technology has redefined the role of the designer by allowing for things that would be either too expensive or physically impossible in the "real" world of wood and wires.

**Are you ready to...**

- Work on new products from inception and design through physical creation?
- Re-imagine existing pieces of equipment, taking a new look at an old item?
- Work with clients to customize creations?

**It helps to...**

- Have an eye for design.
- Be a musician yourself, with an understanding of the intricacies of an instrument.
- Be a strong craftsman, able to work with your hands.

**In high school you can...**

- Take shop classes and graphic design classes.
- Learn by doing: Build your own instruments.
- Help friends and local bands with equipment repairs and updates.

## OTHER MANUFACTURING JOBS

Not everyone who builds instruments needs to be an engineer or designer. There are jobs for people in assembling, finishing, repairing, testing and packaging products. Here are a few examples:

- **ELECTRONICS TECHNICIAN**: Assembles components based on an existing design.
- **WOODWORKER**: Cuts and shapes woods, either by hand or with computer-controlled machines.
- **ASSEMBLER**: Puts components together.
- **LINE MANAGER**: Oversees a section of an equipment factory.
- **FINISHER**: Paints, covers or otherwise puts the final touches on an assembled product.
- **QUALITY CONTROL TESTER**: Before products are shipped, they may undergo rigorous tests to make sure that all of their features are working correctly.

- **PACKAGE DESIGN:** From logos to boxes to in-store displays, package designers are similar to their record industry counterparts: They make sure that the product gets noticed—and leaves the right impression.
- **SHIPPING:** Overseeing the packaging and delivery of products to both consumers and retailers at home and abroad.

## Looking Ahead

As long as there are bands, live performances and music being made anywhere, there will be a need for instruments. While instruments like the guitar, piano and drums have remained relatively unchanged in the last half-century, technological advances continue to influence samplers, outboard gear and effects. This means that there is a market for both traditional and contemporary innovation in musical equipment and instruments. As the music-making process becomes increasingly democratized, and as more and more people begin to make music, the needs of musicians expands tremendously. These needs are met by the innovators in instrument and equipment technology.

# 13

# LEARNING OPPORTUNITIES

There are plenty of immediately available opportunities to start you down the path toward a career in the music industry. This chapter outlines a number of these opportunities, but this list is by no means exhaustive. You should check local universities, music stores, songwriter associations and other resources for programs and events.

Now is the best time for you to begin gaining experience in the industry; aside from the benefits of the learning process, you'll discover the areas you enjoy working in and those you don't. There is also less risk at a young age: You're able to take more chances without the same level of responsibility that you will have later in your career.

# Finding Opportunities

Begin searching for every possible way to get involved with the music business—whether it's volunteering to handle the sound and lighting for a talent competition or attending events at a university music program. Once you start experimenting with your various talents, you'll develop an understanding of your strengths and weaknesses. From there you will develop a better idea of the areas to apply yourself later, when you're beginning your career in earnest.

The number of learning opportunities continues to grow, but this list offers an overview of some of the best examples at the time this book was written.

## GRAMMY CAMPS

The Recording Acedemy runs a number of programs bringing students into contact with industry professionals.

### LA (USC campus) and NY (Converse Rubber Tracks Studio, Brooklyn)

- LA tuition is $2,200, which includes lodging, accommodations, all meals, curriculum and transportation.
- NY tuition is $1,800, which includes lodging, accommodations, meals, curriculum and transportation.
- Combined cost (if you attend both) is $3500 ($500 discount).
- One time application fee of $25.
- Need-based financial aid is available—over 70 percent of those who have applied in the past have received some amount of money.

**Overview of Grammy Camp summer program in LA**

- LA = 10 day program of total music immersion.
- Each student comes on a certain track: songwriter, vocalist, instrumentalist, audio engineer, electronic music production, music journalism or concert production/promotion.
- You work with other students to ultimately create an album of new music to which every track has contributed.
- Classes, rehearsals, field-trips and concerts/lectures centered around guest artists.

**Summer program in NY**

- Seven days of total music immersion.
- Each student will participate in a specific career field: music business and production, singer/songwriter, or performance (instrumental or vocal).
- Students are put into teams that take a music project from its inception to a launch party held at Best Buy Theater in Times Square; process goes from promotion and marketing to final product.
- Classes, rehearsals, field-trips and concerts/lectures centered around guest artists.

**Grammy Camp: Basic Training**

- One-day sessions that take place in high schools, colleges and universities throughout the country—no tickets sold, you just have to be a student at the school where the camp is taking place.

- Interactive sessions with artists, music attorneys, managers, concert promoters and digital marketers.
- Educators can apply to have their school included.

### Grammy Camp: Sound Check

- Introduces you to an artist and someone from the artist's team (manager, booking agent).
- Past artists have included Dave Matthews, Coldplay, U2, Kanye West and John Mayer.
- Educators can apply to have their school included.

## NEW YORK UNIVERSITY

### The Clive Davis Institute of Recorded Music:
### Future Music Moguls

- For high school freshmen, sophomores and juniors.
- A free workshop held on Saturdays starting in February and ending in May.
- 12 to 15 students are selected for the program.
- Students learn about: writing hit songs, producing records, marketing music, managing artists, music for mobile, financial literacy, money management and business skills.
- Applicants must demonstrate: strong interest/participation in music or business leadership, academic achievement, ability to work as a team member, willingness to collaborate a firm commitment to completing all 12 workshops.

**Steinhardt: Music Business Summer Institute for High School Students—New York**

- One-week program: Each day of the institute has a theme that teaches you about the music business, ranging from A&R scout and performer to record label executive and manager.
- The tuition is $1190, plus $370 for housing and meal plan fees.
- There are two sessions during the summer.
- Must be 16 years old by late June in order to be considered.
- Contact the program director, Catherine Radbill, at 212-998-5427 or info.wmas@gmail.com.

## DREXEL UNIVERSITY

**Music Industry Summer Program—Philadelphia, PA**

- One-week program where students take three courses Monday through Friday from 9:30am to 4:40pm.
- Courses include: digital audio production, the new music business models, songwriting workshop, audio engineering, publishing industry, online social media and marketing workshop.
- The director is Marcy Rauer Wagman, once Creative Direction of FCD, Inc. and serves on the Board of Governors of NARAS.
- Open to high school students, at least 16 years old, who have completed their sophomore year by July.
- Tuition is $1200.

■ Contact the summer program coordinator at 215-895-1834 or tjm22@drexel.edu.

## P'TONES RECORDS

This non-profit after school music program for at-risk high school students provides opportunities in the music industry.

■ Locations in Brooklyn, Durham, Tallahassee, DC, Atlanta, LA, Manhattan and Miami.

■ Full-service recording studios in urban communities; mentors work with students in hands-on studio environments.

■ Follows a six-course curriculum: multimedia, A&R, publicity, marketing, art and new media.

■ Culminates in each student's composition, production and mastering of a complete album.

■ Spokespeople include: Nas, Talib Kweli, Kevin Durant, Lil' Wayne and many more.

■ High school seniors in the program have opportunities to receive full scholarships to partners like Florida A&M and N.C. Central University as well as internships in the music industry (Warner Music).

■ Contact info@ptonesrecords.com.

## PROJECT RYTMO

**Reaching Youth Through Music Opportunities—Anaheim, CA**

■ Non-profit after-school program for youth.

■ Program is comprised of four comprehensive courses;

studies include music history, music theory, commercial songwriting, digital recording, beat-making, production, vocal exploration, instrument lessons, audio engineering and more.

- Full course tuition (four courses) is $1,200. If you're low-income, however, you may qualify for a scholarship.
- One course = $350, one course half scholarship available = $175, one course full scholarship = $45.

## MCNALLY SMITH UNIVERSITY

### Summer Camps—St. Paul, MN

- MIX: Music Industry eXperience
- One week program that includes workshops, music business presentations, experience with recording technology, creation of sound tracks, musical performances and more.
- Hip-hop Workshop.
- Run by Sean McPherson (bandleader of Heiruspecs), the camp connects attendees with Twin Cities emcees, producers and graphic artists.
- Focuses on hip-hop production, history and performance.
- Instructors lead demonstrations, hold Q&A sessions and have hands-on sessions in the recording studios; concludes with a final performance—ages 13 and up.
- Contact Sean McPherson at smcpherson@mcnallys-mith.edu or call 800-594-9500.

■ Registration fee = $400, lunch fee = $60, housing fee= $400, airport pickup = $50.

## ORPHEUS

### Neutral-Zone for Teens—Ann Arbor, MI

■ Free after-school workshops for teens.

■ Workshops include: B-side promotion, DJ workshop, emcee workshop, beatmaking workshop, open music lab, b-boying workshop and more.

■ To reserve a spot in the course, email carlos@neutral-zone.org.

## MUSICIANS INSTITUTE

### 'Summer Shot' Program—Los Angeles, CA

■ Intensive six-day programs that are offered in either performance, recording, songwriting or guitar building.

■ Must be at least 14 to apply—some prior music study is recommended.

#### PERFORMANCE:

■ Six hours of instrument-specific classes, two one-hour sessions with an instructor, evening 'open jams,' counseling sessions with musicians to ask questions/jam, seminars on style, technique, music business and songwriting. See concerts, record a live performance on DVD with a band that "matches your age, style, and experience."

**RECORDING:**

■ Six hours of hands-on recording that covers session set-up, loops and beats, file management, MIDI sequencing, production, mixing and mastering, Pro Tools, Reason and more. Daily clinics with engineers; labs are open after sessions to work on projects and practice. Finish the week by working in MI's SSL 4000G+ Tracking Studio; create a final project that you showcase at a listening party.

**SONGWRITER:**

■ Art and craft of songwriting, including theory for songwriters, melody writing, lyric writing, rhythm and groove, creativity workshop, songwriter's circle and private lessons.

■ Business of songwriting: how to sell your songs and panel discussions about music business.

■ Performance: open mic, rehearsal, end the week with a concert in a 500-seat concert hall—recorded on DVD.

**GUITAR BUILDER:**

■ Learn to: cut the body from wood using CNC technology and shape the details, design and cut the headstock, finish the detail in the body/neck, wire and install pick-ups and electronics, install hardware and set up/fine-tune guitar to pro specs.

■ You get to take home the guitar you've made and assembled at the end of the week.

■ To request an application, call 1-800-255-7529.

## ITHACA COLLEGE

**Summer College for High School Students—Digital Music Production—Ithaca, NY**

- Music recording using Pro Tools: Students learn to use Pro Tools in a professional recording studio environment under Brian Dozoretz (has worked on albums from Wyclef Jean to Tony Bennett to Interpol).
- Course requires no prior experience in either music or recording.
- The course counts as college credit (student's future university may or may not accept it as transfer credit though, depending on their music department).
- $25 application fee, space is limited to 12 spots.
- Tuition for one-week session = $1,280; three-week session = $4,280.
- Brian Dozoretz contact info: bdozoretz@ithaca.edu or (607) 274-1603.

## BERKLEE COLLEGE OF MUSIC

**Five-Week Summer Performance Program—Boston, MA**

- All instruments, all contemporary styles and all levels of musical ability.
- Immersed in all aspects of performance: classes, workshops and rehearsals. Play in ensembles, develop improvisation and reading skills, weekly private lessons and lectures/demonstrations by faculty and visiting artists.

- Various tracks are: jazz, pop/rock, funk/fusion and pop/R&B.
- Application fee is $50.
- Total tuition is $4,420, housing payment is $150, housing fee is $3,075, registration fee is $35, comprehensive fee is $150.
- Students can apply for scholarships, but they are limited and and intensely competitive.
- Contact 617-747-2245 or summer@berklee.edu.

**Berklee in Los Angeles, CA**

- Students work through processes of writing, producing and marketing a song from conception to completion. Classes in songwriting production, recording techniques, performance techniques, music business and electives (like sheet writing, audition techniques and improvisation).
- Five-day program, must be at least 15 to apply and have at least one year of experience in music.
- Application fee is $50.
- Tuition is $1175.
- Contact 617-747-2245.

**Twelve-Week Full-Credit Program**

- Earn a full semester of credits.
- To apply, you must be 16 years old with a minimum of two years of formal music training/experience and good working knowledge of music theory.
- Classes include: private instruction (one 30 min lesson

per week), instrumental/vocal labs or ensembles, ear training, harmony, introduction to music technology and writing/arranging skills.

■ Tuition = $12,350, comprehensive fee = $610, housing deposit = $300, residence hall fees = $7,060, tuition payment = $100, application fee = $50 (total = $20,470).

### Other Berklee Programs

**STAGE PERFORMANCE WORKSHOP:**

■ Three-day workshop on song selection, musicianship and your 'look'/how to present yourself.

■ Tuition= $595, housing = $370, application fee = $50.

**SONGWRITING WORKSHOP:**

■ Three-day workshop featuring courses in singer/songwriter workshop, music composition for songs, lyric writing, creating your own demo and recordings, business of songwriting and concerts.

■ Tuition = $790, housing = $450, application fee= $50.

**BUSINESS OF MUSIC:**

■ Two-day workshop: seminars and workshops on business, legal and technological issues affecting record companies, music publishing, talent management and concert promotion.

■ Tuition = $580, housing = $300, application fee = $50.

**VIDEO GAME SOUND AND MUSIC WORKSHOP:**

■ Three-day workshop that explores the creative/technological aspects of sound and music for video games; opportunities to attend professional-level video game scoring sessions.

- Tuition = $595, housing = $370, application fee = $50.

**VOCAL SUMMIT:**

- Three-day workshop that teaches vocalists how to prepare, rehearse and lead a band; offers training in pop, rock, R&B, country, gospel, jazz and musical theater.
- Tuition = $595, housing = $370, application fee = $50.

**PIANO/KEYBOARD WORKSHOP:**

- Develop skills in ensemble playing, improvisation, performance, chord theory and synth technology.
- Everyone participates in one of the following electives: synthesizer performance, jazz master class, hammond class or new age music improvisation.
- Tuition = $790, housing = $450, application fee = $50.

**MUSIC PRODUCTION WORKSHOP:**

- Weekend workshop with topics like: scoring to picture, critical listening, multimedia authoring, audio and MIDI production, business of music production synth programming, desktop digital audio, multitrack recording techniques, mixing techniques, etc.
- Tuition = $1,425, housing = $370, application fee = $50.

## WAGNER COLLEGE

### Summer Music Theatre Institute—Staten Island, NY

- Two-week intensive, professional acting and musical theater training.
- Tuition is $3200, no scholarships are available.
- Not all participants need previous formal training, only a drive to learn about their craft.
- Classes and trips to Broadway; at the end of the program the students perform in a show.
- Students can receive college credit for an additional fee of $250.

## INTERLOCHEN

### Summer Camps—Interlochen, MI

- Multi-week summer music programs include: orchestral and wind ensembles, vocal arts and operetta, vocal soloist studies, jazz, piano, organ, harp, classical guitar, composition, audio recording, singer-songwriter and rock.
- One-week instrumental institutes include: bassoon, advanced bassoon, advanced oboe, cello, clarinet, flute, trombone, trumpet, percussion and horn.

#### AUDIO RECORDING:

- Two-week program, open to students from grades 9-12. Covers fundamentals of audio recording (microphone design, digital audio, recording systems and signal flow, careers in audio, the recording business, etc.).

- Includes lectures, sound-playback, discussions and hand-on demonstrations.
- No audition is required, but applicants must have a minimum of two years playing experience, their instrument and the ability to read music.
- Tuition = $2,935.
- Faculty includes Alan Bise (Azica Records, Thunderbird Records) and Bruce Egre (Cleveland Institute of Music).
- Email admission@interlochen.org or call 800-681-5912.

**SINGER-SONGWRITER:**

- Two-week program to develop skills on guitar or piano and voice. Students create a portfolio of ideas and lyrics for new songs—includes group sessions, performance opportunities, and 'coffee house' style concert performance.
- Tuition = $3,020.
- Audition requirements: video-recorded personal performance of an original composition with a written copy of the lyrics.
- Email admission@interlochen.org or call 800-681-5912.

**COMPOSITION:**

- Six-week program: students will have their compositions performed by musicians in chamber groups.

Twice a week students have private composition lessons. Seminar in compositional techniques and music theory class.

- Audition requirements: two compositions (audio files optional), resume that includes primary instrument, years of study, list of compositions written and performed and description of any formal training in composition.
- Tuition = $7,315.
- Contact camp.iterlochen.org.

## OTHER OPPORTUNITIES

### Digiwaxx Internship Program

- Independent marketing and promotions agency specializing in urban lifestyle.
- 15-20 hours in Midtown Manhattan office.
- High school students are welcome to apply.
- Job responsibilities include: administrative duties, blogging regularly, managing social media outlets and updating mailing list.

### Follow Your Dreams, Inc.—Baltimore, MD

- Youth-run recording studio for at-risk kids where students can learn from their peers about recording and producing music.
- Contact 410-366-1092 for more information.

### Belmont University Summer Camp—Nashville, TN

- Five-day summer camp for stringed instruments
- Tuition = $700

### Eastman School of Music—Rochester, NY

- Two-week program with classes in theory, history of music, performance, ensembles and private lessons
- Tuition = $1,750 or $3,115 with housing and meals.

### Juilliard Summer Percussion and Summer Jazz Workshops

- Percussion workshop is a 13-day program
- Jazz workshops are week-long programs held in locations around the world—FL, GA, UT, Australia.
- Tuition = $1,415

## Looking ahead

Thanks to distance learning, iTunes University, and other electronic apps, educational opportunities are sure to increase over the next several years. Do your research and you should be able to find something that fits any area of the music business you want to explore!

# INDUSTRY INSIDERS

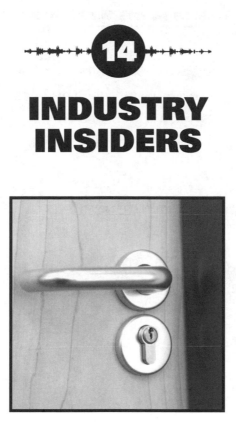

**D**espite their diverse backgrounds and histories, all of the people discussed in this chapter have a passion for music, a love of the social environment that this business fosters, a strong sense of self-motivation and an entrepreneurial spirit. The most successful people in all sectors of the music industry are intellectually curious and are always looking for ways to improve business productivity.

Regardless of your skills and interests, your job in this industry begins and ends with the music—with a ton of hard work in between. In this chapter, you'll read anecdotes, advice and other tidbits from people at the top of their fields.

These career paths and direct quotes grant you access to stories that are otherwise unavailable. This book's insider perspective will give you a leg up when thinking about future careers by providing insight into how those before you achieved success.

## Josh Abraham: Producer
**CO-OWNER** PULSE MANAGEMENT

Abraham's credits include Alkaline Trio, 30 Seconds to Mars, Velvet Revolver, Staind, Limp Bizkit, Linkin Park, Courtney Love, and Static-X.

**How he got started:**

"I figured that maybe if I just helped other bands around town, that would lead to me being an engineer or a producer. In the beginning it was just a hobby. Whether a project did well or didn't do anything, it didn't matter. Everyday we were in the studio it was great."

**The routine of a producer:**

"I talk to all of my writers and producers, deal with all the executives and return every call, every day. Listen to music every day, listen to songs that come in every day. Go through new material."

**Best piece of advice:**

"Return everyone's call."

# Chris Alderman: Tour Manager

**Biggest surprise:**

"How small Nashville is, as far the music community goes. Everybody knows everyone and there's some attachment to somebody whether it's with another band or management company. It's like an amoeba."

**The value of college experience:**

"I went to University of Massachusetts, Dartmouth. I was a business major, which involved accounting, and I was vice president of my class. We organized different acts that came to our school to play. The social aspect of college integrated me into the music industry."

**The music he works with:**

"There's got to be some passion for the music you represent, whether it's as a manager or as a crew guy."

# Jim Anderson: Engineer/Educator
**PROFESSOR** NYU CLIVE DAVIS INSTITUTE OF RECORDED MUSIC

**How he got started:**

"I had an immense curiosity about electronics and about how music and electronics interacted. I was constantly ripping apart radios and record players. There were no programs where you could put all this together though. When I graduated from high school, the option was to go for a music degree."

**How to be the best:**

"You want to get to the point where you're beyond technique

and everything becomes natural to you. When you sit down and you go to listen to what you set up, it should be exactly what you had imagined in your mind."

## Steve Armstrong: Musical Instrument and Equipment Industry
**DIRECTOR OF MARKETING** PEARL DRUMS

### How he got to Pearl Drums:

"I played drums in high school and college and marched on the drum line at Murray State. My focus was always to work in the advertising field. I had grown from being a one man advertising department to getting hired by MCA Records in Nashville to be their director of marketing. Terry, the President of Pearl, was looking for a marketing person to come down from NY. I played drums in the past and that's how I ended up in Pearl."

## Gary Arnold: Marketing Executive
**FORMER SENIOR VP OF ENTERTAINMENT MARKETING** BEST BUY

### From selling flowers to selling records:

"I was in college, and it was music that made me feel more fulfilled than anything else I had been involved in. In school I needed a way to pay for tuition, so I got a job delivering flowers. A woman gave me a dollar tip, and I remember saying to myself, 'I'm going to spend all of my tips every day on music, on records.' As I did my route every day I scheduled a stop at one record store, so after doing this for a long period of time, I asked the people at the record store for a job, and they gave me one."

**To be successful:**

"You have to be a pitcher. By that I mean, if you wait around for someone to bring you a great opportunity, it will never show up. You need to plug yourself in and be listening."

**The best advice he's received:**

"The reality is that it's so hard to be found, you have to work harder than the next guy—and in today's world it's even further amplified. There are so many highly talented people out there that being found is where the hard work starts."

# Ron Broitman: Film/TV Licensing
**SENIOR VP AND HEAD OF SYNCHRONIZATION** WARNER/
CHAPPELL

**Making the transition from law to music:**

"I was the first in the family to go to college, and much less an Ivy League law school. Music took a back seat, and it was really about entering the world and making my mark. In my very brief two years of practicing law, I was unhappy; I was working insane hours without really caring about the work. I probably wasn't the best young lawyer even though I was a good law student because it didn't mean anything to me.

It really became clear after a conversation with my old world Russian dad. I said, 'I love music, I've played in bands, I think the music business is where I need to be. I think I can use my law degree and my brain. I know I'm a good thinker, I love music, and I can put the two together.'

I didn't know what that meant at the time, all I knew was that I didn't want to be a lawyer. I knew that you had to start as an assistant to do something more creative. My father, pounding his fists on the table, was furious: 'I did not bring you to this country to be a secretary.'"

**Taking risks:**

"I had a skill set, I had some tools—the academic, the music, the legal—I didn't know what to do with them, I didn't know where I'd end up, and it was all very scary. I had massive law school debt and was out on my own—after walking away from a law firm job and being unemployed by choice—to make a new life and get into the business."

## **Barbara Cane**: Performing Rights Organization Executive
### VP, GENERAL MANAGER WRITER-PUBLISHER RELATIONS BMI

**Role of college education:**

"It isn't the major or the graduate major that you declare; it's being in an academically challenging environment that sets a standard of responsibility for us individually to complete, do our best and deliver. I think those are the components and qualities that one carries when one transitions from school to career."

**How she got into music:**

"What steered me to my career was my dad, who is retired now but was in the music business. His passion, his mentorship—I idolized the pure enjoyment that he had publishing music and managing artists, which impacted me in my pursuits and decisions."

**To be a great executive:**

"You must love music, love writers, love going out at night, get along well with people and integrate into a team. But the flip side is, you have to understand the responsibility, the administrative component, and learn to manage that. Those go hand in hand with making a great executive."

## Troy Carter: Artist Manager/Entrepreneur
**MANAGER AND FOUNDER, CHAIRMAN, AND CEO** COALITION MEDIA GROUP

**His best advice:**

"Whenever you can be the good guy, be the good guy. Be big in little things."

**What keeps him motivated?**

"The change that's happening in the music business. Over the next 5-10 years, we're going to see a huge shift and the industry won't look anything like it did 10 years ago. I want me and my team to be on the forefront of that page."

## David Caruso: Marketing Executive
**CHIEF OPERATING OFFICER** UNITED ENTERTAINMENT GROUP **AND CREATOR OF** ACME BRAND CONTENT COMPANY

**Applying his college experience to the music industry:**

"My degree is in marketing and business. I always wanted to combine that with something I was passionate about—combine my book education with something in my heart. I've always been passionate about entertainment, so I asked myself, 'How can I take what I learned in school and make money from it?'"

### Why choose advertising?

"I was a promoter out of college: I was promoting events and dabbling in concert promotion and I thought I liked the excitement of that field, but it was very non-strategic and a little dirty for me. I flip-flopped into the advertising business, which was very strategic and regimented, and I found a balance with the excitement of the music and entertainment business."

### Advice:

"Read a lot. Learn about both sides of business. Speak two different languages [creative and analytical]. When you're trying to bring two sides together, you really have to understand what motivates both sides and know what their agendas are. Best piece of advice: knowing that everyone has an angle and everyone wants something. My job is to know what that something is; finding that common ground is the way that we get things done."

## Angelica Cob-Baehler: Record Executive
**FORMER EXECUTIVE VICE PRESIDENT MARKETING** EPIC RECORDS

### On her early interest in music:

"It started a lot younger than most people: I was maybe 5 years old. I used to go up and sneak into my uncle's record collection and put on big headphones and listen to artists like the Beatles."

### On using the resources at hand in college:

"I didn't have a lot of contact with college music or college radio, but I did discover the career center there and I started doing questionnaires to figure out what my skill set was."

## Maureen Crowe: Music Supervisor
**CO-FOUNDER** PLAN R SOUNDTRACKS

**The beginning years:**
"I did a lot of musical theater growing up. I was a big fan of movies and singing and dancing. I went to school for communications and worked for a television show for PBS called Upstate Travels. I came out to LA and worked on a lot of student films because I didn't know anyone in LA."

**On learning the job:**
"I started talking to publishers and record labels and that's how I learned to do the job. The path is to work with filmmakers, work on movies, work on television shows, work on the internet: that was it. After the television show ended I had worked basically 18 hours a day for four or five years. I was physically exhausted."

**Piece of advice:**
"It's not just who you know, it's who knows you. Put yourself out there."

## Doug Davis: Attorney
**OWNER/PARTNER** DAVIS FIRM

**Learning from a young age:**
"Prior to college, my father gave me no free rides and every summer he'd have me work in an intern position in some ca-

pacity at Arista Records. I was learning all about the business from when I was 11-12 years old."

**Trading politics for entertainment:**

"I wanted to pursue a career in politics. I went to Syracuse where the program is one of the top in the nation. It didn't cross my mind that I wanted to go into entertainment. I worked very closely in the campaign in upstate New York with Bill Clinton and also with Brown while he was running for President. The original goal was a career in politics that I subsequently knew I didn't want to do."

**Who gets the job?**

"It's the ones who work the hardest and are the most aggressive, not necessarily the ones with the best resume."

# Josh Deutsch: Record Executive
**CHAIRMAN AND CEO** DOWNTOWN MUSIC LLC

Deutsch previously worked in A&R at Capital Records with such artists as Gnarls Barkley, Cold War Kids, Jason Mraz, Justice, Santigold, Jet, Lenny Kravitz, Third Eye Blind and Megadeath.

**The importance of high school:**

"Where I went to high school there was an electronic music program that was very advanced. Between what I learned at the studio at our high school and summer internships through recording studios as a high school student, I was really prepared for some of the opportunities in college."

**Biggest challenge:**

"The big frustration is trying to manage the inflow and out-flow of communication. Mind you, that's the best problem in the world to have. And I'm very grateful to have that problem. Time management is critical in this type of job."

**Advice:**

"If you want to be in the music business, get in somewhere and then outwork everyone else and over-perform. Someone told me as a young A&R person to reinvent myself. That advice has been something that I've carried with me broadly through Downtown—we feel an urgent need to innovate."

## Serona Elton: Educator
**PROFESSOR,** UNIVERSITY OF MIAMI, **PRESIDENT OF MEISA**

**Background:**

"When I was in junior high school I remember holding a handful of vinyl records saying that I want to be a label executive. I went to University of Florida, which didn't have any kind of music business program, so I majored in finance. My theory was that finance is about money and every single business involves money, so how could I go wrong in finance? There was a local music video show on the local cable access channel. At the time, they were pretty widespread, so I got involved in the two local video shows. On one show I booked all of the interviews. Even though I didn't go to a school with any music business program whatsoever, I went to University of Miami [for graduate school] and got very involved and was extremely active there. I worked for a local record label and started Caine Records in 1993. I finished my masters at University of Miami and was just about to start law school there when EMI moved me up to New York to work for that year. So I went to law school at night while I worked for EMI."

**On internships and networking:**

"Networking is the perfect opportunity to let people know what you know. Your fellow students are the ones who might help you get jobs eventually. Your working starts while you're in school."

## Tim Godwin: Musical Instrument and Equipment Industry
### DIR. ARTIST AND ENTERTAINMENT RELATIONS TAYLOR GUITARS

**His best advice:**

"Do what you love to do. Ask yourself, 'What do I have a passion about?' It will kind of come to you. If you have a passion for something you really love doing then it's not work and you end up getting paid for it."

**Hardest part of the business:**

"There are times when there's someone you want to help but can't. It's an emotional business, but you can't help everybody."

## Randy Grimmett: Performing Rights Organization Executive
### EXECUTIVE VP MEMBERSHIP ASCAP

Grimmett is also a board member of the Association of Independent Music Publishers.

**Early years:**

"I grew up in rural Oklahoma. From high school I went to the University of Oklahoma and double majored in English and Radio/TV/Film production. I was one of those guys who knew that new records came out every Tuesday; I was always a key discoverer of music."

**From estate lawyer to band manager:**

"When I got into law school, my plan was to go to a law firm that represented banks and did a lot of estate planning. During law school, there were a few things going on in Oklahoma—there was a great folk scene—and it was during that time as a diversion to my law school studies that I started working for a band. From that point I began to manage them and, instead of taking a typical job after law school, I ended up on the road with a band."

**Biggest surprise in the music industry:**

"Despite the fact that I had both an undergraduate and a professional degree, I still had to start at the very bottom."

## Jennifer Howell: Philanthropist
**FOUNDER** ART OF ELYSIUM

Art of Elysium is a non-profit organization bringing actors, musicians and artists to engage with children battling serious medical conditions.

**Her inspiration for the philanthropy:**

"My first year [in LA] I lost a friend to leukemia. And basically he just said not to feel sorry for him but to actually do something for the children who don't have anybody in the hospital. He changed my life by telling me about a little boy who he shared a hospital room with while he was waiting for his second bone marrow transplant. And that was it, I just kind of went in a different direction."

**The biggest surprise:**

"The biggest surprise was that everyone was willing to help. It spreads goodwill and the music community has really embraced the charity because it's so accessible. I thought that I would have more roadblocks than I did."

# Maura Johnston: Journalist
**FORMER MUSIC EDITOR** *VILLAGE VOICE*

Johnston's work has also appeared in Popdust, the Awl, Newsday, NPR and other publications.

**On getting started:**

"I went to Northwestern, which was a very strong journalism school. I worked on the newspaper there but I wasn't a journalism major; I majored in online communication when it was coming up. It was so new and fast moving that I knew I was going to want the internet in my career. I had been freelancing on the side since I was in college.

Having the environment of extracurriculars at Northwestern fed into my dual obsession with music and technology— and also with my passion for writing. I worked at the radio station, which was great for music discovery. I'd just sit in the basement and go through all the new records that had been added to the station's playlist that week.

There was a lot of learning; there were a lot of classes we had to take if we were going to be in the rock program. We had to go every week and find out about these different genres of music. It was really helpful to visualize the sorts of connections bands had and what sort of things I might like."

**Working with your interests:**

"You have to deal with your interests because that makes you curious. Curiosity makes for a better blog post."

## John Kiehl: Recording Studio Owner
**CO-FOUNDER,** THE SOUNDTRACK GROUP

**On gaining experience:**

"I learned that it was OK to be doing things that aren't exactly in line with the lighthouse that you're pointing your life toward, as long as it was loosely in that direction."

**The key to success:**

"There are no clients that are going to come to you as a studio separate than coming to you as a person. Your facility has to be something wrapped around who you are."

**The college experience:**

"I went to MIT because that's what someone in my family was destined to do. I deserved to go to MIT: I had an 800 math score on my SATs, and was obviously a math and science guy. I never found myself at MIT though. I just kept looking around saying, 'I'm not like these guys; it's not my passion.' Upon graduating, I became a musician because that's where my passion led."

## Josh Klein: Financial Manager
**MANAGING DIRECTOR** MONARCH BUSINESS AND WEALTH MANAGEMENT

### The importance of education:
"Education was the most important thing in my career. I got my job from someone that I met during college, and I interned during college for the same company that I now work for."

### Best piece of advice:
"If you make a mistake, own up to it, admit it, find the best solution and come clean. If you don't know it, tell someone you don't know it and be the first to get the right answer."

### What continues to motivate him:
"I have a separate interest in the industry: that I'm a fan. It's not just work for me; it's something that I like to do with my personal time. Even though I'm only on the business side, it's important to know what clients are out there and which ones are profitable."

## Ryan Leslie: Artist
**CREATOR** NEXTSELECTION LIFESTYLE GROUP

In addition to creating NextSelection, a music/media company, Leslie has released albums such as *Just Right* (2005), *Ryan Leslie* (2009) and *Transition* (2009).

**The college experience:**

"I think that the college environment for me was the most valuable piece of higher education. So that meant that first of all I was surrounded by like-minded peers who were all very ambitious and hardworking. That was very, very inspiring. The social microcosm that existed—talent shows, after-parties—gave me a lot of insight into how the real world was going to be working. I took it upon myself to participate in all of those activities and I traveled the world with a singing group, took advantage of a college recording studio that they had. I took advantage of every opportunity I could possibly find to perform original music and now that I'm a decade out of college, most of my peers that I really respected are all very successful in synergistic businesses, whether it's intellectual property, finance or more creative; and now that's also a resource and network that I can tap into."

# Joe Levy: Journalist
**EDITOR** BILLBOARD MAGAZINE

**On starting out:**

"I was really interested in pop culture, and my friend Julian wanted to start a magazine devoted to pop music. We decided to start a campus publication [at Yale] devoted to those things. We named it after a Chuck Berry song, 'Nadine,' for no good reason except that we couldn't decide on a better name and we both loved Chuck Berry. The amazing thing is that publication produced more than its fair share of professional music writers. That magazine actually lived on for 10 years. A lot of my career in journalism has been spent in very strange and interesting transition points. We started this thing when, in order to create a newspaper or magazine, you actually had to have a typesetter. We spent most of our money on the first issue sending out copy to a typesetter. There's really no such thing anymore. By the time we did the second one, Kinkos had a laser printer, and we went there and printed out a column of type."

### How have things changed?

"The easy money isn't there anymore. But the passion for music and the audience—we all know that's completely there."

### Lesson about the business:

"Quality is only one of the things you're selling. Quality is no guarantee of success."

# Doug Nightwine: Tour Manager
**TOUR MANAGER** FOR KELLY CLARKSON AND JASON MRAZ.

### A Memphis education:

"I was a teenager in Memphis, TN. I was a product of the public school system there, and one of the things they provided was training and vocational classes. One of them happened to be a recording class and we went three hours a day to a small recording studio."

### Picking it up and running with it:

"I had just turned 17. By Christmas of that year, I was already mixing crappy bands in crappy clubs on crappy PAs, thinking I knew what I was doing. When summer rolled around, I ended up spending the summer on the road all over the Southeast. It wasn't glamorous, but for a 17-year-old kid it wasn't bad. I chose not to go back to my senior year of high school. I jumped in with both feet, with attitude and assertiveness—people gave me a lot of opportunities because of it."

**The worst part of the gig:**

"Accounting. As tour manager, it's all about the numbers—you have to put all the budgeting together."

## Jake Ottmann: Music Publishing Exec.
**FORMER EAST COAST CREATIVE VP** EMI PUBLISHING

Ottmann is also co-founder of Fingerpaint Records (Beck). At EMI he worked with the Fray, Metro Station, Coheed and Cambria and Boys Like Girls.

**Biggest surprise of working in the music industry:**

"I sort of stumbled into the music industry. The biggest surprise was that you could actually make a living doing this and that all my previous life experience actually served a purpose. Spending my time listening to music, doing anything I could to go watch music—all that stuff actually meant that I could make a living off of music."

**Tough skin:**

"Batting .300 in our business would be great—but I get 'No' about 90 percent of the day. You have to be able to accept the fact that people are going to say no to you. You have to believe in your ideas and your instinct."

## Bob Power: Producer/Educator
**INSTRUCTOR** CLIVE DAVIS INSTITUTE OF RECORDED MUSIC

Power's production credits include Erykah Badu, D'Angelo, Miles Davis, the Roots, David Byrne, Curtis Mayfield, De La Soul, the Jungle Brothers and others.

### On beginning his career in producing:
"I didn't start engineering for other people until I was in my early 30s. It didn't seem like there were obstacles and hurtles just because I loved it so much. The hours were brutal, but everyone has that core of their career for 20 or so years when they work 80, 90 hours a week."

### On the skills needed to be a producer:
"To be a producer you should be someone who really knows music, sonics and engineering, record companies and how to navigate through them. You should be someone who has an urge to do saomething creative, however primitive your music skills."

### The challenges of being a producer:
"To do a reality check on one's self to make sure one's personal preferences musically are not getting in the way of the artist."

### What's still exciting about being in music?
"What motivates me now is exactly the same thing that motivated me when I was 14: a real passion and interest in the music. And I happen to love helping people as well."

# DJ Rekha: DJ
**INDEPENDENT ARTIST, FOUNDER** BEAT BAZAAR MUSIC

### Artistic inspiration:

"I was born in London, England and grew up in Queens and Long Island. I listened to a lot of Indian music at home and a lot of American music. There was also a lot of underground electronic music on radio. I grew up when hip hop was born—growing up in a middle class black background in Queens exposed me to a lot of fresh music. I got into DJing, scraped some nickels together and bought a sound system. I had no idea I'd do this professionally. I didn't choose it, it chose me. You do art when you can't not do it. If you have to think too much about it, you probably shouldn't do it."

### Creating her own niche:

"I created something because what was available didn't satisfy me. My desire was to create a party that I wanted to go to and combine the two musical genres that I like the most."

# Rick Sackheim: Record Executive
**EXECUTIVE VP** ISLAND/DEF JAM

### Role of education in a career:

"I graduated from UC Berkeley, political science major, and when I first got in the record business I really felt like it played no role in what I was doing at all. And now that's it been 20 years, looking back, it was the best thing for me because an education—no matter what background your studies are in—is only going to benefit you in some capacity or another. So when I was younger, I felt like it didn't play a role. And now that I'm older, I'm so happy I did it. And I wish I could get a Masters."

### How he manages his time:

"It's multitasking at all times—it starts off with the biggest fire to the smallest fire and then, when it comes to trying to actually getting things done, the big fires come first. Once you put out all the fires you can put your right foot forward. But the thing is, there's always a fire somewhere to put out."

### How does his music taste affect his work?

"I think that good music is good music. Taste, for a real music person, isn't just pigeon-holed to one genre. Music lovers should love all types of music."

## Chris Sampson: Educator
**ASSOC. DEAN DIV. OF POP MUSIC & INDUSTRY STUDIES**
USC THORNTON SCHOOL OF MUSIC

### The role of education:

"Education was central to my particular experience because my education—particularly within a university environment—allowed me to understand the culture and climate that goes into a higher education learning atmosphere."

### On his educational path:

"I studied at USC, where my degree happened to be in classical guitar performance. My route to that major in that school was unusual. I was a rock drummer for a band that did some touring and performing on the East Coast. I knew I wanted to attend school as a music major, so I taught myself just enough classical guitar to fool them and pass my audition."

## Michael Solomon: Artist Manager
**CO-FOUNDER** BRICK WALL MANAGEMENT

### First job with the Boss:

"My first job was touring with Bruce Springsteen. I was seeing how things are when they are perfect. That's not always the best starting point. My experience working on that tour was traveling in private planes and staying in the nicest hotels in the world: it was in the lap of absolute luxury. That was a dangerous place to start."

### The importance of college:

"By going to college, you have every competitive advantage. In this day in age, you have to have a fall-back plan, and your college degree can be your passport to doing something else."

## Ron Spaulding: Distribution Executive
**FORMER PRESIDENT** FONTANA DISTRIBUTION

### Finding your niche:

"When I grew up I thought that everyone in the music industry had to be a performer. I started at $3.35 an hour in overnight stock at a main department store company and later ended up becoming an assistant buyer for that same chain in music, movies and books.

I learned that there were a lot of people involved in the music business that didn't stand on stage every night, so I said, 'Let me see if I can't find an area in the industry that I might be good at.' That area happened to be sales."

### What's important?

"The key is that you have to develop a good balance between the creative aspect and the business aspect."

### Best advice:

"A very important notion of fairness has to factor into how you do business. It's not always about getting the highest dollar."

## Steve Stoute: Marketing
**FOUNDER** TRANSLATION CONSULTATION AND BRAND IMAGING

### Path to the industry:

"1990, 1991, there was a big push between record labels buying content from street artists and hip-hop artists, and if you were around it and you had the ability to get those artists off to the record labels, there was a job there."

### From labels to advertising:

"I went through the system, going up the ranks and always being curious. I figured out the role that advertising and commercials played in the record business. Being interested in the advertising industry allowed me to take some of the holes that existed in the record business and advertising business and fill them in."

# **Danny Strick**: Music Publishing Executive
**CO-PRESIDENT** SONY ATV

### On his formative years:

"Being in madrigals and glee club in middle school was amazing. We used to perform, my mother playing countless musical soundtracks, all those kinds of things combined. I had an extreme love for music, obviously the burgeoning music scene living in LA. In terms of Southern California bands, being able to go to places like the Troubadour, the Roxy, the Whiskey on a regular basis. As I grew up, the Ash Grove, amazing... also I worked in record stores starting in college, I worked for record stores after college, I worked a number of years at record stores."

### How did college prepare him?

"I think probably only in the sense of interacting with people; not really from an academic standpoint. I think that if I had to do it over again, I might have taken business classes and done some different kinds of things outside of the liberal arts."

# TODAY, TOMORROW AND BEYOND

**W**ith constantly evolving technology and plenty of advances in the digital space, there is more opportunity than ever before to create and define your own path within the music industry. Though many people have pointed toward the digital age as something to compete with or struggle against, it is far more useful to determine the benefits of these changes. The widespread availability of technology has, in many ways, democratized access to creating music and participating in the music business. With far more ways to become involved in the industry, the boundaries that once defined the traditional major label systems have been shattered.

Certain changes may hurt one segment of the music business while also benefiting another by opening new opportunities. Gone are the days of sending out resumes and waiting to be discovered. The relationship between artist and fan has never been more fully connected. Bands can explode through their social media presence, musicians can connect by sending recorded files to one another and artists can distribute their music to fans across the world with incredible ease.

Young executives with great ideas may very well find themselves holding the next big industry breakthrough. Building that idea into a profitable business model has never been easier; decades ago it took years to build companies, brands and artists. Now it takes less than a year. Youth is at the forefront of technological innovation, and with music and technology inextricably linked, the music business is finding many of its most creative and lucrative answers from young leaders.

In the earliest, most primitive stages of recorded music—a time when sheet music publishers and performers made up most of the 'music industry'—emerging forms of technology were not taken seriously as threats to the contemporary landscape of music. Rather than preparing for change (and much less embracing it), sheet music publishers felt that the success of their industry would remain consistent. Why pay attention to Thomas Edison and a talking machine when they were making thousands of sales, right?

We know what happened to sheet music—just like we know the history of tapes and CDs. But did the music industry die with the seismic shift from sheet music to recorded music? Of course not. Instead of focusing on products that have been passed over, we should focus on the innovation that occurred to replace them. With the advent of the digital age, the landscape of the music industry certainly shifted—but for young, talented, entrepreneurial people, the digital age has opened up endless possibilities.

Regardless of music's medium—whether digital, vinyl, live, 8-track, boom box or otherwise—both the art and the music business remain vital, thriving and internationally present. This field is special because it allows you to get up close with those individuals who are actively creating great work and influencing cultures on a worldwide basis.

When you work in the music industry, you have the ability to collaborate with artists. Even on the smallest, most remote scale, you have had a part in the artists' success and you have helped spread his/her music to people across your town, across the US or across the globe. If you're passionate about the artistic medium in which you work, that passion enriches your own life while also helping to bring a cultural icon to the forefront of others' lives. When you get to participate in the success of something you love, it's a dream come true.

It's students like you who are going to shape the music industry of the coming decades. Some of you will influence the business directly, while others will shape it in more subtle ways. You don't have to become an executive at a major label, manage a Grammy-winning act or develop the next huge tech breakthrough to have an impact. You can write liner notes, help independent bands market themselves, supervise the music for television commercials or do anything in between. The industry is a synchronized dance: There are tons of moving parts—some of which may get more recognition than others—but they are all important, and they all work together to create a final product that we can enjoy.

This book's insight into the various jobs of this industry should not just be used just to narrow down your own career future. You should also do your best to become an encyclopedia: The more you know about what others do, the more you will have an appreciation for their role in your success and your role in theirs. In order to work effectively and efficiently with others, you should have a clear idea of what they do and what you need to be doing. This mutual understanding will make both of your jobs easier and will produce better results.

There's no one correct path to success in the music industry. A lot of the jobs discussed in this book are interconnected, and a lot of the skills critical to one position bleed through to another. Marketing, for example, takes similar forms whether you work for a publisher, a label or an instrument company. Marketing music is marketing music. It is not uncommon to see a seemingly non-linear career path with many different jobs at many different companies. Oftentimes these jobs are related and connected in important ways. It is very possible to be successful in the music business by being good at many different things, without ever fully becoming an expert at one.

Of course, there are jobs like radio promotion where you spend years cultivating important relationships and know-how. These jobs require an expert skill set. But oftentimes, when you see people running their own companies, they have more diverse backgrounds. From A&R to marketing to radio, some are entrepreneurs and some are managers. It's important to get your foot in the door anywhere that you can. In the music industry, it's just as important to figure out what you don't want as it is to figure out what you do.

## THE FUTURE OF ENTREPRENEURSHIP

I hope that this book has enticed you with its introduction to the many great jobs available in the music industry. However, the one job it has failed to address as of yet is the job that you create for yourself.

As the music landscape continues to evolve, there is great opportunity to launch your own music business venture. New music related start-ups are popping up every day, and emerging technology is exposing uncharted territory to fresh innovation.

There are infinite ways to find and consume music in today's industry climate. With that increased accessibility and distribution comes the opportunity to better the user experience by finding easier ways to deliver music and music-related merchandise. The possibilities for innovation are endless.

## GET STARTED NOW

If you're waiting for an opportunity to break into the music business, you're going to be left behind. As in so many other industries, competition is fierce—but that shouldn't be discouraging; it should motivate you to work harder than anyone else. You cannot wait for your chance. Instead, you need to take as much initiative as possible to put your ideas into action, get your name out and begin gaining as much experience as you can. It's possible to get a head start by beginning to actualize your ideas *now*. Based upon the information that you're learning here, start formulating your plan of attack. Where do your interests lie? What are your skill sets? The wonderful reality of starting now is:

A) You're starting early and will gain crucial experience.

B) There's little price for failure: Now is the time that you can take risks, try new things and experiment without endangering your long-term success.

C) You will meet like-minded peers and start forming relationships that may be beneficial later in your career.

Start a music blog, design your band's album artwork, help a local indie artist book gigs around your town, manage social media for an upcoming singer/songwriter; the opportunities are virtually endless to help prepare you for years to come.

When passion and talent meet hard work, great results are bound to follow: Use your abilities and motivation to their fullest extent and, with some time and experience, you'll carve out your own niche in the music industry. Whether you want to headline a world tour, write album reviews for your favorite publication or teach eager college students, your work begins now.

# PHOTO CREDITS

# NOTES

# NOTES

# NOTES